A CONSPIRACY OF DECENCY

**Other Westview Press books
by Emmy E. Werner**

Pioneer Children on the Journey West, 1995

Reluctant Witnesses: Children's Voices from the Civil War, 1998

Through the Eyes of Innocents, Children Witness World War II, 2000

A CONSPIRACY OF DECENCY

The Rescue of the Danish Jews
During World War II

Emmy E. Werner

Westview
PRESS

A Member of the Perseus Books Group

Copyright © 2002 by Westview Press, A Member of the Perseus Books Group

Westview Press books are available at special discounts for bulk purchases in the United States by corporations, institutions, and other organizations. For more information, please contact the Special Markets Department at the Perseus Books Group, 11 Cambridge Center, Cambridge MA 02142, or call (617) 252-5298.

Published in 2002 in the United States of America by Westview Press, 5500 Central Avenue, Boulder, Colorado 80301–2877, and in the United Kingdom by Westview Press, 12 Hid's Copse Road, Cumnor Hill, Oxford OX2 9JJ

Find us on the World Wide Web at www.westviewpress.com

A Cataloging-in-Publication data record for this book is available from the Library of Congress.

ISBN: 978-0-8133-4278-8

The paper used in this publication meets the requirements of the American National Standard for Permanence of Paper for Printed Library Materials Z39.48–1984.

10   9   8   7   6   5   4   3   2   1

Cover photo: Relief by sculptor Harald Isenstein honoring the rescue of the Danish Jews. Town Hall of Helsingborg, Sweden. (Courtesy of K. E. Ander, photographer)

For Stanley Jacobsen and Olof Lidin,
Hanna Duckwitz, and Hanne Schulsinger,
and in memory of John Meilstrup Olsen

Contents

Contents

List of Illustrations

Maps

Acknowledgments

For this book I relied on the help of many people of good will from five different countries. It was indeed a "conspiracy of decency" that made it possible for me to locate persons, photos and documents in Denmark, Sweden, Germany, Israel, and the United States. My thanks for their generous assistance go the following individuals:

In Denmark

Mogen Adelson, Isak Berkowitz, Jette Borenhoff, Dan Edelsten, Leon Feder, Ulf Haxen, Anita Melchior, Bent Melchior, Hanne Meyer, Ove Nathan, Kirsten Meyer Nielsen, Henning Oppenheim, Allan Philip, Herdis Rosenbaum, John Saietz, Fini and Hanne Schulsinger, and Freddie and Silja Vainer, who shared their experiences during and after World War II.

Also, Eva-Maria Jansson, Center for Orientalia and Judaica, Royal Library, Copenhagen; Charlotte Lang, Jødisk Pædagogik Center, Carolineskolen, Copenhagen; Olof Lidin, Professor Emeritus, University of Copenhagen; Henrik Lundbak, Assistant Curator, The Museum of Danish Resistance, Copenhagen; Jan Nielsen, Archivist, Rigsarkivet, Copenhagen; Mrs. Inger Meilstrup Olsen, Copenhagen; and Lone J. Runitz, Researcher, Danish Center for Holocaust and Genocide Studies, Copenhagen.

In Sweden

K. Erik Ander, photographer, Helsingborg; Marianne Cederblad, Professor Emeritus, University of Lund; Rolf Kjellman, Consul,

Royal Danish Consulate, Helsingborg; and Hanne Trautner-Kromann, Jewish Studies, University of Lund.

In Germany

Hanna Duckwitz, Winsen/Aller; D. Doringhoff, Bundesarchiv-Militärarchiv, Freiburg im Breisgau; and Elisabeth and Hans Strubelt, Bremen.

In Israel

Shaul Ferrero, the Holocaust Martyrs and Heroes Remembrance Authority; and Dr. Mordecai Paldiel, Department of the Righteous Among Nations, Yad Vashem, Jerusalem.

In the United States

Phyllis B. Bishof, Librarian, University of California, Berkeley; Carole Blair, University of California, Davis; Karen Cantor, Washington, D.C.; Barney Cohen, Archivist, Holocaust Center of Northern California, San Francisco; Paul Victor Ghysels, Berkeley, California; Anne Ipsen-Goldman, University of Minnesota, Minneapolis; Marilyn Ibach, Reference Specialist, Prints and Photograph Division, Library of Congress, Washington, D.C.; Mette Shayne, Chicago; Christopher Sims, United States Holocaust Memorial Museum, Washington, D.C.; Ulla Thomsen, Novato, California; and of course, my husband, Stanley Jacobsen, Berkeley, California. Thanks also to Rob Williams, Steve Catalano, and Barbara Greer at Westview Press as well as to Marian Safran for all their help along the way.

Emmy E. Werner

Prologue

The people of Denmark, a small country at the northern tip of the European mainland, managed to save almost their entire Jewish population from extinction in a spontaneous act of moral courage that has no equal in the history of World War II. I would like to tell the story of the rescue of the Danish Jews from the vantage point of eyewitnesses, both Gentiles and Jews. Most of these eyewitness were children and teenagers at the time. Today, they are among the last survivors of an extraordinary conspiracy of decency that took place in the midst of the horrors of the Holocaust and World War II.

This book chronicles the acts of people of goodwill from several nationalities. Among them was Georg F. Duckwitz, the German shipping expert who warned the leading Danish politicians of the German plans for a forced deportation of the Jews; members of the German navy who placed their ships in dry dock, so that Danish fishing boats with their Jewish cargo could pass unharmed across the Øresund; teenage members of the Danish resistance movement and Danish policemen who assisted in the rescue and in the armed struggle of the underground, and physicians and Red Cross workers who looked after the Jewish children and their families after they found refuge in neutral Sweden.

Chapter 1 opens with the invasion of Denmark by German troops on April 9, 1940, and chronicles the slow but steady growth of passive resistance and individual acts of defiance by the Danes against the occupation forces in 1941 and 1942. The eyewitness accounts are those of grade school children from Copenhagen and provincial towns in Jutland and on the isle of Funen (Fyn). The chapter includes an account of the first organized acts of sabotage by members of the Churchill Club—eleven teenage boys from Aalborg—who were arrested, tried, and jailed in the spring of 1942. It ends with the imposition of martial law by the German occupiers and the resignation of the Danish government in August 1943.

Chapter 2 deals with the events set in motion after the representative of the German Reich, Werner Best, sent a telegram to Berlin on September 8, 1943, requesting police support for the arrest and deportation of the Danish Jews. Georg Duckwitz, the German maritime expert, when told about the telegram, flew to Berlin and made an unsuccessful attempt to intercept the fateful message before it reached Hitler. On September 28, when informed about the date of the pending deportation, Duckwitz passed on the news to leading members of the Danish parliament and to the Swedish ambassador in Copenhagen.

Eyewitness accounts of the actions of the German diplomat are contained in his diary in the archives of the Foreign Ministry of the German Federal Republic in Berlin, in his memoirs in the archives at Yad Vashem in Jerusalem, in the Danish National Archives in Copenhagen, and in his daybook. They are supported by the testimony of Swedish and Danish politicians deposited at Yad Vashem.

Chapter 3 tells the story of the spontaneous outpouring of Danish support for their Jewish compatriots in the wake of the events of late September 1943. The Danish bishops issued a letter of support for the Jewish community that was read in all Lutheran churches, and the universities in Copenhagen and Aarhus closed down in protest. By the time the roundup of the Jews began on October 1, the Danes had succeeded in hiding almost their entire Jewish population and in moving them to coastal ports for their escape to Sweden.

The eyewitness accounts in this chapter are those of students, nurses, and doctors who hid Jews in hospital beds (as well as in morgues and funeral corteges!), of Danish fishmongers, housewives, and teachers who provided a hiding place for their Jewish neighbors in their homes, and of Danish fishermen, policemen, and members of the underground who hid fleeing Jews in fishing sheds and warehouses in Copenhagen and other coastal ports.

Chapter 4 describes the journeys of the Danish Jews to safety across the Øresund during the first two weeks of October. It is based on eyewitness accounts from twenty-five successful crossings. The voices are those of Jewish children and teenagers, their Danish rescuers, members of the Swedish coast guard, and the captain of a German patrol boat. In his memoirs, Georg F. Duckwitz paid special tribute to the harbormaster of the port of Copenhagen, who saw to it that the coastal patrol vessels of the German navy were placed in dry dock for repairs—precisely at the time when the rescue operations began. By mid-October, 7,220 Danish Jews had been saved.

Chapter 5 deals with the efforts of the Swedish authorities and many individual citizens to provide a decent asylum for the refugees, most of whom settled in the harbor towns of Helsingborg, Malmö, and Göteborg, as well as in Lund and Stockholm. It is based on Swedish newspaper accounts of the time and on eyewitness accounts of Swedish public health officers and policemen who met the refugees upon their arrival. It also includes interviews with former students of schools in Stockholm, Göteborg, and Lund. The university town of Lund was home to the largest school for Danish refugee children, who continued their studies under the tutelage of Danish teachers, with Danish textbooks smuggled across the Øresund.   *education*

Chapter 6 tells the story of 461 Danish Jews, 40 of them children, who did not make it to Sweden, but were apprehended by the Gestapo and sent to the Theresienstadt Concentration Camp in Bohemia. They were finally released in April 1945 and brought by Red Cross buses to Sweden. The man primarily responsible for this mission of mercy was Count Folke Bernadotte, a member of the Swedish royal family. About 90 percent of the Danish inmates of Theresienstadt survived.

This chapter includes the eyewitness accounts of a teenage boy and of a five-year-old girl who was transported with her father and pregnant mother from Copenhagen to Theresienstadt. Together with her one-year-old brother (who was born in the camp), she returned safely to Denmark after a brief stay in Sweden. Among those who returned alive as well was "Aunt Clara," the widow of an admiral in the Danish navy who was in her eighties and nearly deaf. She returned with her indomitable spirit—and her hearing trumpet—intact.

Chapter 7 tells of the events that escalated the Danish resistance against the German occupation forces in 1944. Among the eyewitness accounts are the voices of two teenagers who lived in Copenhagen. Both were in hiding. One survived; the other perished. The survivor was a Jewish girl who stayed with her mother under an assumed name in her apartment—protected by members of the Danish police, the Danish resistance movement, and by neighbors, teachers, and fellow students who did not betray her new identity. Today she is professor emeritus of clinical psychology at the University of Copenhagen.

The other was a Danish merchant seaman who had been deeply troubled by the treatment of the Jews and who had decided to fight their oppression. He joined the underground movement in 1944 and was arrested and sentenced to death in April 1945, ten days before the end of World War II in Europe. A portion of his diary and letters to his mother and girlfriend were found hidden in the walls of his cell in Vestre Prison in Copenhagen, where he was tortured and executed.

Danish Jews were not the only Danes to be sent to German concentration camps. In 1944, many resistance activists, Danish policemen, and other Danes deemed "undesirable" by the Gestapo were transported to camps in Germany. By the end of the war, there were 6,000 Danish prisoners in camps like Buchenwald and Neuengamme, including 2,000 policemen. Ten percent died. Among the survivors was a young university student, Jørgen Kieler, who was arrested for acts of sabotage, and a Danish policeman, John Meilstrup Olsen. The latter's Christmas letter to his wife and infant daughter from Buchenwald and Kieler's Christmas greetings to his mother lend a special poignancy to this chapter.

Chapter 8 tells of the liberation of Denmark and the homecoming of the Danish Jews. Admiral Dönitz, Hitler's successor, negotiated the surrender of German troops in Denmark on May 4, 1945—four days before the unconditional surrender of the Wehrmacht in the rest of Europe. The early capitulation of the German troops saved Denmark from a final orgy of destruction and made it possible for 250,000 German refugees to return to their homeland unharmed. Toward the end of May the Danish Jews began to return from Sweden. Most found their belongings intact, just as they had left them eighteen months earlier. Their homes and apartments had been cleaned and painted, their pets and gardens had been cared for, and their neighbors greeted them with flowers and "Velkommen til Denmark!"

Chapter 9 tells the story of what happened to the major players in this "conspiracy of decency" after World War II ended. Werner Best was tried by a Copenhagen court and served six years in prison. Georg F. Duckwitz remained in Copenhagen and became the first ambassador of the new Federal Republic of Germany to Denmark. In 1971, a tree was planted in his honor in the Avenue of the Righteous at Yad Vashem in Jerusalem.

As a gesture of gratitude for the rescue of their Jewish citizens, the entire country of Denmark was recognized as "Righteous Among the Nations" at Yad Vashem. Many Jewish children and teenagers who were saved by their fellow Danes are now among their country's most prominent citizens. They regard their rescue as the ultimate expression of human decency.

Chapter 10 considers the lessons we might learn from this unique event in the history of the Holocaust and of World War II, and from the individual acts of moral courage of thousands of ordinary people whose names are now honored as "Righteous Gentiles" at Yad Vashem. It explores the roots of the rescuers' altruism and caring. Regardless of their nationality, social class, level of education, or religious and political persuasion, they shared *one* important characteristic. They defined their humanity by their ability to behave compassionately. They did not consider their actions heroic—they simply thought it was the decent thing to do.

1

❧❧

Shadows over Denmark

In Churchill Park in Copenhagen, not far from the statue of the Little Mermaid, is the Museum of Danish Resistance. Its entrance is guarded by an armored vehicle used by resistance fighters in the last days of World War II. Inside the museum is a permanent exhibit that tells, in documents and pictures, the story of Denmark between the years of 1940 and 1945.

It's a story worthy of a Hans Christian Andersen tale—warts and all. It tells of the encounter of a small country whose people valued being free and *hyggelig*—cheerful, comfortable, and cozy—with a Giant from the South who one day goose-stepped across their cobbled streets and wanted to turn them into pet canaries. It is a story filled with adventure and intrigue, with tragedy and comedy. Above all, it is a story of human decency.

The story begins at dawn, on April 9, 1940. Most of Denmark was still asleep. In about two hours, between 4:00 and 6:00 A.M., its nine hundred years of uninterrupted freedom and independence would come to an end.[1] The first call to the Danish General Staff Headquarters from the frontier expressed concern about a "heavy noise of engines" along the passage from Rens to Arentoft. The second telephone call, at 4:30 A.M., reported that German troops had

7

crossed the border at Krusa (in Jutland), and five minutes later the Danish Naval Command announced that German soldiers had disembarked at Assens, Middlefart, and Nybørg (in Funen, or Fyn) and were coming ashore at Korsor (in south Zealand, Sjælland in Danish). A German merchant ship carrying an assault battalion had moored at the Langelinie in Copenhagen. By 4:32 A.M. the commander in chief of Denmark's armed forces was awakened in his residence at the Kastellet (Citadel) and told to report to the War Ministry. There he learned that the king and his ministers were meeting at Amalienborg Palace to discuss the German demand for capitulation.

By the time the general had reached Amalienborg Palace, soldiers of the Danish Royal Guard were firing upon German troops in the Palace Square. The Citadel had fallen into German hands by 5:00 A.M. At 6:00 A.M. the German demand was agreed to by the king and his ministers, and the king ordered a cease-fire at the Palace Square. General Prior returned to the War Ministry and ordered the armed forces throughout Denmark to cease all further resistance.

Altogether, thirteen Danish soldiers had been killed and twenty-three wounded that day in skirmishes with German troops in south Jutland and Zealand. No Danish naval vessels or shore batteries opened fire on German troop ships, which were in easy range of Danish naval guns. The navy suffered not a single casualty. In an abortive attempt to defend the military airfield at Værlose, near Copenhagen, one Danish fighter plane was shot down and the rest destroyed on the ground.

The people of Copenhagen awoke that morning to find the streets crowded with German troops and squadrons of German planes circling above the city. Anne Ipsen, who was four days shy of her fifth birthday, remembers in her book *A Child's Tapestry of War* (1998) her parents and herself standing by their living room window, looking up at the German planes overhead. Her father, a physician who was in the Reserve Medical Corps, buckled the leather belt of his army uniform and went downstairs to get a newspaper.[2]

When he returned to their third-floor apartment, bounding up two steps at a time, he told his family, "The newsboy said, 'Hey, Pops, you better get out of that uniform—we've been invaded.'" His daughter recalls that he thought of reporting to the army hospital for orders, but given the circumstances, he decided to take off his uniform. By the end of the day, he was dismissed from any further service in the army. His uniform was hung in the back of the closet.

Denmark had been neutral in World War I and was the only Scandinavian country to sign a nonaggression pact with Germany in 1939. From the earliest days of World War II it had done nothing to protect itself against a possible German invasion. Along the border, no defense fortification had been built, and no preparations had been made to mine bridges or block roads. The fourteen thousand men who made up the Danish defense force had not been mobilized.

The Germans assured the Danish government on the morning of April 9 that "in accordance with the good spirit that has always prevailed in Danish-German relations, the Reich's government declares . . . . that Germany does not intend now or in the future to interfere with Denmark's territorial integrity or political independence." The German commander in chief sought to allay the fears of the Danes by dropping leaflets from the air and broadcasting appeals over the Danish radio. He reassured them that the German forces would "secure the continued existence of the Kingdom, the maintenance of the Army and Navy, respect for the freedom of the Danish people, and the full security of the future independence of this country."[3]

The Danish government, faced with the presence of a German military that was claiming to protect Denmark's territorial integrity, set about a policy of negotiation, trying to find ways to accommodate the invader as well as to assure the safety of its citizens. King Christian X made a personal appeal to his fellow Danes and called on them to "show an absolute correct and dignified behavior." In the beginning, most Danes followed their king's exhortations, but the prevailing mood of bewilderment soon began to change.

Arne Sejr was a seventeen-year-old schoolboy living with his parents at Slagelse, in western Zealand. Throughout the first day of occupation, on April 9, he wandered around his hometown, observing the

Danish officers at German headquarters in Copenhagen. (Photo courtesy of the Library of Congress, Prints and Photographs Division)

behavior of the people in the streets. He was shocked by the friendly way in which many Danes treated the German soldiers, talking to them and even applauding the German military band that was playing Danish music in an open-air concert. The front pages of the local newspapers carried a message from King Christian telling his people to behave like good Danes.[4]

Arne asked himself, "How does a good Dane behave in a situation like this, when his country is occupied?" He wrote down his answers under the heading "Ten Commandments for the Danes" ("Danskerens 10 bud") and typed out several copies:

1. You must not take work in Germany or Norway.
2. You must do worthless work for the Germans.
3. You must work slowly for the Germans.
4. You must destroy important machines and gear.
5. You must destroy everything useful to the Germans.
6. You must delay all transports.
7. You must boycott German and Italian newspapers and films.

8. You must not trade with Nazis.
9. You must deal with traitors as they deserve.
10. You must defend everyone persecuted by the Germans.

JOIN IN THE FIGHT FOR DENMARK'S FREEDOM

On the evening of April 10, he pushed copies of his ten commandments through the letter boxes of some of the most influential citizens of his hometown—the mayor, bankers, doctors, journalists, and local politicians. "I felt very illegal," he remembered, "ducking through the dark streets where the only sounds were made by the hobnailed boots of the German patrols."

Acts of passive resistance and *"den kolde skulder"* (the cold shoulder)—a method the Danes adopted to show their contempt for the Germans—began to multiply in the years to come. Gradually the Danes became unfriendly, rebelling in the only way they knew, by avoiding the soldiers whenever possible. Anne Ipsen would learn some valuable lessons in "passive resistance" when she accompanied her mother on shopping trips in downtown Copenhagen.[5]

One day on the way to buying bread, they stopped halfway down the block when her mother saw two German officers going into the local bakery. Anne noted that the customers inside the store left and waited outside until the soldiers departed with their whipped cream–covered cakes. Then the Danes entered the store and bought their bread. Eventually, the Germans stopped going to the local bakeries, disconcerted by the frigid courtesy at the counter and the emptying stores.

When Anne traveled with her mother on the streetcars in downtown Copenhagen, she noticed a similar incident. The streetcars had open platforms on the front and back for standing passengers. Sliding doors separated these open areas from the compartment with the seats. At one stop, German soldiers climbed on the streetcar, slid the door open, and sat down in a crowded compartment. By the next stop, the compartment was almost empty, but the platforms at the front and back were packed with standing passengers. Eventually the soldiers got off, and the Danish passengers sat down. Soon the Germans preferred standing in the cold air on the platform to the chilly reception inside the streetcar compartments.

Children in the rural area of Denmark also learned to ignore the soldiers or to keep a distance from them. Christian Søe was in the first grade when German troops were stationed in his hometown in eastern Jutland. "My childish reaction was one of general astonishment rather than fear over the many uniformed men with military trucks, motorcycles, and horses," he recalled later. For a long time he and the other children in his small town had no direct contact with the invaders. "Always say '*nicht verstehen*'—I don't understand"—he was told by his elders.[6]

One of Christian's favorite songs was a parody of "Lily Marlene":

> *First we take Goebbels by one of his legs,*
> *Now we take Göring and beat him with a stone,*
> *Then we'll hang Hitler from the noose,*
> *Right next to Herr von Ribbentrop,*
> *The big Nazi swine, the big Nazi swine.*

Ridicule was a common way to express one's defiance against the invaders—whether you were a child or an adult. One evening at a Copenhagen theater, a Danish comedian looked down at the front row. It was filled with German officers, who had taken the best seats in the house. He began his act by snapping his right arm forward as if in a Nazi salute. The Germans leapt to their feet, saluted the stage, and shouted, "Heil Hitler!" The comedian paused, kept his arm straight out, and said softly, "This is how high the snow was last winter in Copenhagen."[7]

Another story that made the rounds described a traffic post the Germans had set up at a main intersection in the capital. Inside a waist-high circle of sandbags stood a lone soldier, directing traffic. One morning, as the streets filled with people, walking and bicycling to work, a laughing crowd surrounded the hapless soldier. Traffic halted and, finally, an SS (*Schutzstaffel*, the Blackshirts) car arrived. A black-uniformed officer got out of the car and tore down a sign that some-one had tacked up on the traffic post. It read (in Danish): "Attention! This soldier is not wearing any trousers!"

For three years, occupied Denmark managed to maintain a degree of independence and remained an island of plenty and relative peace, unlike any other place in occupied Europe. For the average Dane, life continued near normal, except for the *mørklægningsrullegardiner*—the blackout curtains—that now covered their windows at night to deter the planes of the British Royal Air Force from accidentally dropping bombs on Danish property. The Danish army and navy were not dis-banded. Churches and business and social groups operated freely. Schools remained open. Jobs were plentiful. The income of the Danish farmers rose because of their extensive food exports to Germany.[8] Denmark had become, in Winston Churchill's words, "Hitler's canary" and, in Hitler's words, "the model [Aryan] protectorate."

It even had its own version of Hitler's Nazi party—the Danish National Socialist Workers' party (DNSAP), headed by Fritz Clausen. He had taken over the leadership of the party in 1933, at the time Hitler came to power. His party carried less than 2 percent of the vote (31,000 votes) in the 1939 election, just sufficient to win three seats in the Danish parliament. Support for the DNSAP came mostly from the German minority in southern Jutland. The Danish public did not rally behind them. Several months after the invasion, Clausen (and the Germans) suggested that members of the Danish Nazi party should become part of the government. The king rejected the idea.[9]   Nazi = minority

On September 26, 1940, King Christian's seventieth birthday, hun-dreds of thousands of Danes gathered at the square in front of Amalienborg Palace to cheer him as a symbol of national unity. The king played *his* part in strengthening the morale of his people. At eleven o'clock every morning, he rode, bolt upright in the saddle, through the streets of Copenhagen.   hmm

He acknowledged the greetings of the Danes with a salute, a hand-shake, or a smile, but he never responded to the salute of the German soldiers who sprang to attention as he passed. According to one

Nazi headquarters in Copenhagen (Courtesy of Library of Congress. Prints and Photographs Division.)

often-told story, a puzzled German asked a boy standing beside him on the sidewalk, "If this is your king, where is his bodyguard?" The boy replied proudly, "We are *all* his bodyguards."

During the war a rumor surfaced in England that the Danish king had countered German demands for anti-Jewish legislation by threatening to wear the "Star of David" in protest. Christian X never did such a thing, yet the welfare of the Danish Jews was of great importance to the king and the Danish government. From April 1940 to August 1943, the Danish Jews led lives free from fear of harassment

King Christian X riding his horse through the streets of Copenhagen during the German occupation. (Photo courtesy of the Museum of Danish Resistance)

or arrest. At no time was the wearing of the Star of David one of the German demands in Denmark.[10] *only Danish Jews*

The Danish government, however, helped *only* the Danish Jews. From 1933 on, many Jews tried to escape to Denmark from Germany and other countries, but Denmark had a very restrictive refugee policy that made it difficult to get a visa or work permit. The Jewish refugees were either turned back at the border or given temporary resident permits for three to six months and expelled after their permits expired.[11] Many German Jews seeking refuge in Denmark after November 9, 1938, *Kristallnacht*, when Jewish stores and synagogues were ransacked and burned and Jews were beaten throughout Germany, had to try to find safety elsewhere.

An exception was the Youth Aliyah children, who were sponsored by Danish women's organizations that had taken the initiative to help hundreds of German-Jewish children come to Denmark. Their parents, unable to come themselves, sent off their oldest children, hoping they would eventually reach Palestine.

Pursuing a precarious policy of "accommodation," the Danish ambassador in Berlin assured the Ministry of Foreign Affairs that he was doing nothing to help German Jews. But there was a price to be paid for maintaining Denmark's relative peace and freedom. As the occupation continued, German demands began to escalate.[12]

As early as July 1940, three months after the invasion, the Danish government, under pressure from the Germans, curtailed the country's free press. In January 1941, Denmark turned over eight new torpedo boats to the German navy, and in June 1941, after the German invasion of Russia, the Danish government broke off diplomatic relations with the USSR, outlawed the small Danish Communist party, and arrested the three Communist members of the parliament.

Men of military age were recruited for the *Frikorps Denmark*, which was to join the Germans on the Eastern Front. About 8,000 Danes between the ages of seventeen and thirty-five volunteered. They were assured that they would be transferred to the regular Danish army after the war and would receive pensions for their service. They were first sent to Germany for combat training and there received SS uniforms, weapons, pay, and allowances. Then they were sent into action in Russia.

They suffered heavy casualties. All told, about 3,900 Danes lost their lives fighting *with* the Germans—a higher number than the total of Danish losses in the fight *against* the Germans (3,172). The first commander of the *Frikorps*, a Danish artillery officer, was killed in one of the early battles (near Saint Petersburg). The officer appointed to succeed him, Christian Schalburg, a Russian-born Dane who was a lieutenant-captain in the Danish Royal Guard, was killed two weeks later. Henceforth the *Frikorps Denmark* would bear his name.

On November 25, 1941, again under German pressure, Denmark signed the Anti-Comintern pact, which was aimed at the USSR. The pact proclaimed a joint struggle with the Axis nations (Germany, Italy, and Japan) against international communism. Most of the top ministers in the Danish government felt that the signing of this pact infringed on Danish neutrality. Danish students staged a protest in the streets of Copenhagen against the government's "policy of negotiation." The demonstrations lasted several days and had to be broken up forcibly. Jørgen Kieler, a medical student who later would become active in the resistance and rescue movement, was one of the youths who were beaten up by the police.

The Danish ambassador in London resigned in protest. Two weeks later, the United States entered the war. Henrik Kauffmann, the Danish ambassador in Washington, promptly signed, on his own initiative, a formal treaty with the United States, placing the Danish colony of Greenland under U.S. protection. Greenland would provide a strategic base for the American armed forces. He resisted an order from Copenhagen to give up the Danish embassy and remained in Washington. *more resistance*

Back home, the Danish public was beginning to embark on a more active path of resistance, stirred on, in part, by students who were publishing underground newspapers and engaging in individual acts of sabotage, and, in part, by the news broadcasts and exhortations of the British Broadcasting Company (BBC). The BBC had an avid listening audience in Denmark, where many people understood English, and among the German soldiers who were stationed there. Christian Søe, who was in the third grade at that time, has vivid memories of three older and partly invalid German soldiers who were stationed in his hometown. They would regularly visit his mother, who served as an occasional translator, and listen with her to the evening news, because they trusted London more as a source of reliable information than Berlin.[13] *V campaign*

In 1941, the BBC, through a Danish-speaking member of the broadcast section, Leif Gundel, introduced the V campaign:

Vi har V'et, det gode, gamle, danske V, der staar for Vilje til agt Vinde—
For Vejen til Sejr—for Varslet om arvefjendens endelige sammenbrud—
For den gamle Vikingeånd—V'et der betyder at VI Vil VINDE.

[We have the V, the good old Danish V, which stands for the Will to Win,
For the Way to Victory—for the warnings of the enemy's final collapse,

For the old Viking spirit, the V that means *We Will Win.*]

The Danes seized upon the V campaign with enthusiasm. The letter began to appear wherever there was a blank space on the wall. Beethoven's Fifth Symphony became a favorite selection on the Danish radio: Its opening bars duplicated in musical terms the Morse code for the letter V—dot, dot, dot, dash.

The conservative newspaper *National Tidende* printed an advertisement for a commercial business that began with the following lines, "Vi Vil Vinde mange kunder i kraft af vore billige priser og vor extra prima Expedition." Even the German censor could not object against this statement, for it merely meant, "We will win many customers through our low prices and first-rate service."[14] But the Danes understood and smiled. What they lacked was an accurate picture of internal events and informed comments on international events. The underground newspapers *De Frie Danske,* first published in the fall of 1941, and *Frit Denmark,* launched in the spring of 1942, began to fill this need.

Anne Ipsen was in the second grade in 1942 and able to identify the banner head on the thin bunch of papers that would be dropped in the mail slot or left on the window sills of their apartment. "*Frit Denmark* is here," she would yell. Her father admonished her. "The newspaper is printed by the Underground, and we and the person who delivered it will get in a lot of trouble if the Germans hear you." "What's the Underground?" she wondered. Copenhagen had no subway at that time, but the little girl imagined dark tunnels and caves under the city where the newspapers were printed.[15]

By the end of 1942, Arne Sejr—the author of the "Ten Commandments for the Danes"—was a university student. He and his friends published a newsletter, *Studenternes Efterretningstjenste* (the students' information service), from an apartment house that was a student hostel. Other underground newspapers were printed in attics and basements, and in the office of a dentist. Before the German administration commandeered all the rooms of Dagmarhus, in the Copenhagen Town Hall Square, an illegal newspaper was even printed on a duplicating machine in the subbasement, while German type-writers clattered upstairs!

The "illegal" press had access to a steady stream of people who were willing to write, print, and distribute the newspapers, and to accurate news provided by the BBC in London, the Danish Press Service in Stockholm, and the Danish ministries. Most of all, it had hundreds of thousands of faithful readers: There were 552 underground newspapers, which printed more than 23 million copies during the occupation. The largest source of income was from the sale of banned books. One of the best-sellers was even printed in German—a pocket diary containing detailed instructions in the reference section on how to feign illness. A doctor's prescription was reproduced that the German soldiers could copy and present at any Danish pharmacy shop to get "medicine" guaranteed to induce some form of incapacity![16]

The prescription form was popular among the German soldiers, because some were older and invalid, and others had been wounded on the Eastern Front and sent to Denmark for R and R (rest and recreation). Thousands of copies of *Führerworte* (The Führer's words), a critical collection of quotes culled from Hitler's speeches, were distributed among the German troops stationed in Denmark. One of the other best-sellers printed by the underground press (in Danish) was a cookbook with recipes for homemade explosives and grenades. It sold briskly once the resistance movement began to hit its stride in the spring of 1942.

One of the first organized sabotage groups was the Churchill Club. Its eleven members were teenage boys, ranging in age from thirteen to seventeen. Knud Pedersen, one of the founders, wrote about the boys' escapades in his book *Churchill-Klubben* (1945). He and his brother Jens had formed the club early in the occupation, at Odense, where their father was a Lutheran minister. The family moved to Aalborg (in north Jutland) at the end of 1941, when Pastor Pedersen was appointed to a post at the Cathedral. The two brothers were sent to the Aalborg Cathedral School and lost no time in reorganizing the club there. They began operations early in 1942.[17]

One of their new members was Uffe Darket, who later became a pilot with the Scandinavian Airlines (SAS). The members began to collect weapons in the hope that they would be able to join the liberating forces when they arrived from Great Britain. Uffe remembered:

> Getting guns was no trick at all. . . . We'd accost soldiers after a parade or at a railway station and while a couple of us engaged them in friendly conversation, the others would steal the rifles they propped against a wall or bench. Our best hunting grounds were the restaurants. The German officers hung their belts and holsters in the cloakrooms and we would pinch the pistols from them. The local barracks was another good spot. . . . While they were in their huts, polishing their equipment or busy with other chores, we'd lift their rifles through the open windows.

The Churchill Club in Aalborg carried out about twenty-five sabotage actions. Their biggest job was the burning of a freight train loaded with military supplies. They had made friends with the German guard by running errands for him. He told the boys about the contents of each wagon. Their youngest member—in the best Boy Scout tradition—set fire to one wagon with only one match. Soon the whole train was ablaze.

The boys also burned down barrack sheds of local Danish collaborators who worked for the Germans. Once they found an unguarded truck. The youngest in the group struck a match, peered into a tank, and said: "Hold on! There's petrol here." They stuck a rag into the tank and lit it and the truck burned. "We were too young to understand the risk we were taking," concluded Uffe Darket.[18]

Their game came to an end on May 8, 1942, when they were arrested. A cloakroom attendant had pointed them out to the police, suspecting they were petty thieves. They sat in the local jail in Aarborg for two months. On June 11, they were tried and convicted, given sentences ranging from one and one-half to three years. Andres Nielsen (age 13), the boy with the matches, was considered underage and was let free.

The teenage members of the Churchill Club arrested in spring 1942. (Photo courtesy of the Museum of Danish Resistance)

Newspaper accounts quoted one of the convicted boys who said, "If you older folk will do nothing, we will have to do something instead!"

They were sent to Nybørg Prison. "When term started, we got on with our school work in jail," reported Uffe. "We had an hour's tuition in the morning, and two hours in the afternoon, followed by two hours of private study in the evening. Scholastically, we probably did better than we might have done in the classroom, because in our cells we had no distractions and no option but to concentrate on our work."

By the fall of 1942, the German authorities were becoming increasingly dissatisfied with the situation in Denmark. A diplomatic crisis erupted following a rather terse telegram from the king, thanking Hitler for his effusive greetings on the occasion of Christian X's seventy-second birthday. (The telegram read, "My utmost thanks, Christian Rex.") Hitler, enraged by the chilly reply from the king, replaced the German diplomat Cecil von Renthe-Fink with SS General Werner Best as head of the German occupation administration, and sent a new "tough" commander in chief of the Wehrmacht, General Hermann von Hanneken, to Denmark.

Best and the German authorities *did* allow a general election to be held on March 23, 1943. A record 89.5 percent turnout gave the coalition parties (the Conservative People's party, the Liberals, and the Social Democrats) 93.4 percent of the vote—only 3.3 percent voted for the Danish Nazi party. That spring the mood of the country changed decisively. The Danes were tired of the German occupation. Most important, they had learned from British and Swedish radio broadcasts that the German forces had capitulated at Stalingrad and that the Axis forces had surrendered in North Africa. Now there was every reason to believe that the Allies would be victorious.[19]

From April 1943 on, strikes and sabotage actions against German transports and installations spread to Danish factories and shipyards working for the German navy. The first major strike began on July 28 at Odense, where a German minesweeper was being built. Two days before the ship was due to leave the shipyard, it was sabotaged. German troops marched into the shipyard, and all the workers walked out. In turn, the workers at every Odense factory and industrial plant laid down their tools. A few days later, a walkout at Esbjerg (in Jutland) at a fish warehouse developed into a "people's strike." All shops closed their doors; all work stopped. The Germans ordered a curfew. The people ignored it. There were clashes with German soldiers on the streets. A couple of days later, the trouble spread to Aarhus, Aalborg, and practically all the towns in Jutland and Funen.

A German officer was sent to Odense to investigate the disturbances. As he walked out of the train station he was met by a jeering mob. Frightened, he drew his pistol and fired six shots, wounding a few people, including a young boy. He was overwhelmed by the crowd and beaten to a pulp.

The most spectacular act of sabotage happened at the Forum exhibition hall in Frederiksberg, just northwest of Copenhagen, after the Germans had hired Danish construction workers to convert the hall into army barracks. On August 24, 1943, the day before the first troops were to move in, a young Danish delivery boy pedaled through the rear entrance of the Forum at lunchtime, when the Danish workers had left the site for their midday meal. In the low underslung carriage of his bike, he carried what looked like a case of Tuborg beer. In reality it contained more than one hundred pounds of explosives.[20]

The delivery boy unloaded the case at a preselected location and pedaled back out. Minutes later two members of the *Holger Danske* resistance group, dressed as laborers, placed the explosives in key locations, set the fuses, and made their escape, undetected. The explosion that followed pulverized the Forum's cement-block wall and left only the steel skeleton standing. For days afterwards, Copenhagen residents bicycled to Frederiksberg to gaze in awe at the naked skeleton that once had been Scandinavia's largest exhibition hall. Holger Danske, the legendary Danish hero who rose from his sleep whenever his country was in trouble, would have been proud of this act of defiance. Four days later, on August 28, 1943, the Danish government was faced with an ultimatum. It was issued by the German administrator in Denmark, Werner Best—under orders from Berlin:

The Danish government must forthwith proclaim a State of Emergency throughout the whole country. The State of Emergency must proclaim the following measures:

1. Public meetings of more than five persons are prohibited.
2. Any form of strike or any form of support of strikers is prohibited.
3. Any form of gathering or meeting in a closed room or in the open air is prohibited. There will be a curfew between the hours of 8:30 P.M. and 5:30 A.M. All restaurants will close at 7:30 P.M.
4. All weapons and explosives will be surrendered before 1 September 1943. Any encroachment on the rights of Danish citizens as a result of their own or their relatives' cooperation with the German authorities, or relationships with Germans, is prohibited.
5. There will be a censorship of the Press under German

control.

6. Summary courts will be set up to deal with cases where the above-mentioned decrees are violated to the prejudice of security and order.

Courts

Violation of the above-mentioned decrees shall be severely punished under the laws which empower the government to maintain order and security. Any sabotage and all assistance in sabotage, any defiance of the German Wehrmacht and of its members, as well as continued retention of weapons and explosives after the first of September, will be subject to the death penalty immediately.

The German government expects the Danish government to accept the above-mentioned demands before 1600 hours today.[21]

The Danish government—which for three and one-half years had based its policy on accommodating the Germans—refused the conditions of the ultimatum. A polite reply was drafted; it pointed out that "effectuation of the provisions demanded . . . would ruin the government's possibilities of keeping the people calm, and the government therefore, regrets that it cannot find it right to help in carrying through these provisions."

The response of the Danish government, approved by the king, was delivered by a messenger to Best's headquarters in Dagmarhus at 3:45 P.M., fifteen minutes before the deadline set in the German ultimatum. From Best's headquarters the news flashed to General von Hanneken, who moved swiftly. Telephone communications with Sweden were cut within an hour. At 4:00 A.M. on August 29, a German messenger awoke Danish Prime Minister Erik Scavenius to deliver the general's decree imposing a military state of emergency in Denmark.

At the same time, German troops attacked Danish army garrisons and depots around the country. All told, twenty-six soldiers were killed during the fighting—twice as many as during the day of invasion. The Danish navy, humiliated after its failure to fight on April 9, 1940, followed its commander in chief's "escape or scuttle" order:

more deaths

Twenty-nine Danish vessels were sunk by their own crews and many more heavily damaged. Thirteen others escaped to Sweden.

By the morning of August 29, when the inhabitants of Copenhagen awoke, the Danish army and navy had been neutralized. German guards were standing guard at all important buildings, including Amalienborg Palace, telephones no longer rang, and mail service had been cut off. Radio announcers read the proclamation of martial law: "No gathering of more than five people permitted . . . . Curfew at nightfall. . . . No mail, telegraph or telephone service until further notice. . . . All strikes prohibited and punishable by death. . . . All offenses to be punished by German military courts."

Von Hanneken declared that the king and government had been superseded by the German military authorities as functioning entities. He also decreed that the Danish government must direct all civil servants to continue their work, and that it must then resign. The Cabinet patiently pointed out that it was powerless to order the civil service to continue, as it already had been forcibly replaced. After further deliberation, the Cabinet requested from the king permission to resign. The king chose not to reply. The legal government was now in limbo, and the actual day-to-day administration fell to the civil service department heads, the undersecretaries in each ministry. Incredulous at the idea of law prevailing even in the face of raw power, General von Hanneken was stymied.

On the afternoon of August 29, SS General Werner Best (who was now engaged in a power struggle with the commander in chief of the Wehrmacht over the ultimate German control over Denmark) called a group of journalists to his office. He began by stressing his "devotion" and "patience" in seeking a course of action that would be in the interest of both countries. He concluded, with a tone of annoyance: "Today I must say that to an appalling extent the press is responsible for recent developments. In this ridiculous little country, the press has implanted the belief that Germany is weak. Last night you got your reward."[22]

2

Men of Conscience

In the evening of August 29, 1943, Georg F. Duckwitz, the shipping
expert at the German embassy in Copenhagen, wrote in his diary:
"It has finally happened and here, too, everything has gone to pieces.
One has to try very hard not to lose one's composure and not to
weep. Four years of hard work is for naught—because of stupidity
and unreasonableness. Now the inhabitants of the last country in
Europe will hate us from the bottom of their hearts. It is very difficult to be a German."[1]

Duckwitz had spent many years in Denmark, was fluent in the
Danish language, and had many close Danish friends. Born in 1904
into a cosmopolitan family of merchants in Bremen, he had studied
jurisprudence and economics in Freiburg and Bonn. He first came to
Denmark in 1929 as a representative of the German coffee merchants
Kaffee Haag.

In November 1932, Duckwitz became a member of the NSDAP,
the German Nazi party. The Danish historian Hans Kirchhoff tracked
down his party papers in the Bundesarchiv (Document Center) in
Berlin, which also holds the SS staff archives. But Kirchhoff found *no*
documentary evidence in these archives to support the claim (made

Georg Ferdinand Duckwitz. (Photo courtesy of
Hanna Duckwitz)

first by the Polish Holocaust historian Tatiana Brustin-Berenstein) that
Duckwitz was an officer in the SS.[2]

From 1933 to 1935, Duckwitz served as an expert on Scandinavian
trade in the German Foreign Ministry and then became an employee
of the Hamburg-Amerika Line, the premier shipping line for passengers and freight to North America (whose founder was a German
Jew). In January 1939, he was appointed the company's representative in New York. When the war broke out in Europe in September
1939, he was "lent" by his company to the German Foreign Ministry
and sent back to Copenhagen. There he worked at one time for the
Abwehr, the intelligence unit of the High Command of the German
armed forces (OKW). Many officers of the *Abwehr* were anti-Nazis,

and the head of the unit, Admiral Wilhelm Canaris, was later executed for aiding the conspirators who tried to assassinate Hitler.

At the time of the German invasion of Denmark in 1940, Duckwitz was a small cog among the big wheels of the occupation hierarchy. The situation changed when SS General Werner Best was appointed the German Reichsbevollmächtiger (plenipotentiary) in Denmark in November 1942. Duckwitz was now drawn into the circle of men Best listened to. By all accounts, Best valued Duckwitz's judgment, experience, and wide circle of Danish contacts. It was not uncommon for Duckwitz to be invited for dinner when Best wanted to meet his Danish counterparts under more informal conditions. Duckwitz's Swiss-born wife—in the opinion of her adopted daughter Hanna—was weary of Best and did not trust him. But Duckwitz— according to Hanna—felt he could appeal to Best's "better nature."[3]

The declaration of a state of military emergency on August 29, 1943, and the resignation of the Danish government took Duckwitz by surprise. His wife, Annemarie, writes in her memoirs: "We were both so upset and ashamed that we did not want to show our face on the street. We were cheered by phone calls from our Danish friends who knew how we felt."[4] Duckwitz was even more taken aback when he learned about the contents of a telegram (#1032) that Best had sent to Berlin on September 8, 1943—ten days after martial law had been imposed in Denmark.

The cable ran as follows:

I REQUEST THAT THE FOLLOWING INFORMATION BE PASSED ON TO THE FOREIGN MINISTER:

WITH REFERENCE TO YOUR TELEGRAM NO. 537 OF 4/19/43 AND MY REPORT OF 4/24/43—II C 102/43—I HEREBY BEG, IN LIGHT OF THE NEW SITUATION, TO REPORT ON THE JEWISH PROBLEM IN DENMARK AS FOLLOWS: IN ACCORDANCE WITH THE CONSISTENT APPLICATION OF THE NEW POLICY IN DENMARK, IT IS MY OPINION THAT MEASURES SHOULD NOW BE TAKEN TOWARD A SOLUTION OF THE PROBLEMS OF THE JEWS

AND THE FREEMASONS. THE NECESSARY STEPS SHOULD
BE TAKEN AS LONG AS THE PRESENT STATE OF EMER-
GENCY EXISTS, FOR AFTERWARD THEY WILL BE LIABLE
TO CAUSE REACTION IN THE COUNTRY, WHICH IN TURN
MAY LEAD TO A REIMPOSITION OF A GENERAL STATE OF
EMERGENCY UNDER CONDITIONS WHICH WILL PRE-
SUMABLY BE LESS CONVENIENT THAN THOSE OF TODAY.
IN PARTICULAR, AS I HAVE BEEN INFORMED FROM
MANY SOURCES, THE CONSTITUTIONAL GOVERN-
MENT—SHOULD IT EXIST—WOULD RESIGN. THE KING
AND THE RIGSDAG WOULD ALSO CEASE THEIR PARTICI-
PATION IN THE GOVERNMENT OF THE COUNTRY. IT MAY
BE ASSUMED, MOREOVER, THAT IN SUCH AN EVENT A
GENERAL STRIKE WOULD BREAK OUT, FOR THE TRADE
UNIONS WOULD CEASE THEIR ACTIVITIES AND THEIR
RESTRAINING INFLUENCE ON THE WORKERS WOULD BE
REMOVED. IF MEASURES ARE TAKEN DURING THE PRE-
SENT STATE OF EMERGENCY, IT MAY BE THAT THE FOR-
MATION OF A LEGALLY CONSTITUTED GOVERNMENT
WILL BE RENDERED IMPOSSIBLE AND IT WILL BE NECES-
SARY TO SET UP AN ADMINISTRATIVE COUNCIL UNDER
MY LEADERSHIP. I WOULD THEN HAVE TO LEGISLATE BY
MEANS OF DECREE. IN ORDER TO ARREST AND DEPORT
SOME 6,000 JEWS (INCLUDING WOMEN AND CHILDREN)
AT ONE SWEEP IT IS NECESSARY TO HAVE THE POLICE
FORCES I REQUESTED IN MY TELEGRAM NO. 1001 OF
9/1. ALMOST ALL OF THEM SHOULD BE PUT TO WORK
IN GREATER COPENHAGEN WHERE THE MAJORITY OF
THE LOCAL JEWS LIVE. SUPPLEMENTARY FORCES
SHOULD BE PROVIDED BY THE GERMAN MILITARY COM-
MANDER IN DENMARK. FOR TRANSPORTATION, SHIPS
MUST BE CONSIDERED A PRIME NECESSITY AND
SHOULD BE ORDERED IN TIME. AS REGARDS THE
FREEMASONS, A POSSIBLE SOLUTION IS THE FORMAL
CLOSURE OF ALL THEIR LODGES (TO WHICH ALL THE

LEADING PERSONALITIES OF THE COUNTRY BELONG)
AND THE TEMPORARY ARREST OF THE MOST PROMI-
NENT FREEMASONS AND CONFISCATION OF LODGE
PROPERTY. TO THIS END STRONG OPERATIONAL
FORCES ARE ALSO NECESSARY. I BEG TO REQUEST A
DECISION AS TO THE STEPS I SHOULD TAKE OR WHAT I
HAVE TO PREPARE IN CONNECTION WITH THE JEWISH
AND FREEMASON PROBLEMS.

"DR. BEST[5]

[handwritten: "anti Jewish problem"]

According to his memoirs, Duckwitz was outraged and offered his resignation when Best informed him on September 11 about the telegram. He told Best "in a very heated discussion" that he did not want to have any part of a bureaucracy that would be judged by history as being responsible for such an inhuman action, and he asked for immediate transfer to another post. A few days earlier, he had received an offer to go to Stockholm from his friend, Undersecretary A. Hencke, in the German Foreign Ministry.[6]

Best called Duckwitz back on September 12 and urged him to remain in Copenhagen—so did his Danish friends, who argued that he could do more good in Denmark than elsewhere in the difficult days that lay ahead for his adopted homeland. His wife supported his decision to stay. "She was my best moral support," he wrote later, "willing to go with me through thick and thin. We never regretted our decision."

Duckwitz's pocket diary indicates that he flew to Berlin on September 13. There he contacted Hencke, hoping to intercept Best's telegram before it could reach Hitler. It was too late. Von Ribbentrop, the German foreign minister, had already transmitted the message to the Führer, though with reservations of his own. *[handwritten: tried to stop it, angry]*

In accordance with the order of the Führer that the deportation of the Jews from Denmark should be carried out, Dr. Best was asked how he would execute the transport of the Jews and how many additional police force would be needed for a successful completion of the action.

Dr. Best reported that he needs fifty additional members of the security police for the completion of the action against the Jews. There is no need to increase the ordinary police force, since it has already been reinforced. A ship will be needed to transport at least 5,000 Jews from Greater Copenhagen. The transport of an additional 2,000 Jews can be accomplished by railroad.

Dr. Best points out that the action against the Jews will lead to serious deterioration in the political arena. One can no longer count on a restoration of a constitutional government. There will probably be unrest and a general strike. It is possible that the King and the parliament will no longer cooperate in the governance of the country, and the King may abdicate.

In view of these reservations of the Reichsvertreter in Denmark, I ask for advice as to whether the Führer would like to have the action against the Jews carried out at this point in time. If so, it would be important to carry it out during the present state of emergency.

R.

On September 17, Best received a notice that the Führer had decided "in principle" to carry out the deportation of the Danish Jews. Himmler had been "advised to clarify the technical details with Copenhagen." Duckwitz wrote in his diary that evening: "Dagmarhus is filled with police. The house has changed its ambience. Its exterior corresponds to the interior changes that have taken place."

That same day, German security police, in civilian clothing, had broken into the offices of the Jewish Community Center (the Mosaisk Trosamfund) and taken records containing members' names and addresses. Duckwitz noted that Best seemed uncomfortable in discussing this "careless and hasty" action, and surmised that the information was seized in preparation for hunting down the Jews. In confidential conversations with his Danish friends, Duckwitz uttered his first warnings about the growing danger of an action against the Jews—without being able to point to a specific date at which this action might take place. He pleaded with them to be prepared for all eventualities ("Vorbereitet sein, ist alles, was getan werden kann").

736.

Instruks fra rigskansler Hitler om gennemførelse af deportationen
af de danske jøder.

18. september 1943.

(B) RAM   *Ad II 417 g Rs*

Hat dem Herrn C.St.S. vorgelegen.

Über St.S.
    U.St.S.Pol

    Ges.v.Grundherr
    LR v.Thadden

vorgelegt.

   Der Führer hat angeordnet, dass der Abtransport der Juden aus Dänemark durch-
führt werden soll.
   Der Herr RAM bittet MD Dr. Best um Vorschläge, wie der Abtransport durch-
führt werden soll, insbesondere um Angabe der nötigen Polizeikräfte, damit diese von
ihr aus angefordert werden können.

   "Westfalen", den 18.IX.1943.

          gez. **Sonnleithner.**

Berlin, 18.IX.1943.

          Seeber.

A copy of Hitler's order authorizing the deportation of all Jews from
Denmark. (Photo courtesy of United States Holocaust Memorial, Photo
Archives)

On September 19, Duckwitz learned from Best that Hitler had
decided that the deportation of the Jews should take place during the
current state of emergency. In his diary entry for that day, he writes,
"I know what I have to do." He immediately contacted a Swedish
friend, Legationsrat Niels Eric Ekblad, who was visiting Copenhagen,
and received a visa from the Swedish ambassador to Denmark, Gustaf
von Dardel, on September 20.

The events that took place in the following days can be recon-
structed from the appointments noted in Duckwitz's pocket diary.
They also fit entries in the appointment book of Werner Best, who
saw Duckwitz on September 21, and next, on September 25, after
Duckwitz had returned from Sweden.[8]

On September 21, in the afternoon, after his appointment with Best,
Duckwitz went to Sweden—under the watchful eyes of the Gestapo.

He was accompanied by Ekblad. According to her diary, Annemarie Duckwitz stayed that night with a Jewish friend, Liselot Morescu.

A meeting with the Swedish prime minister, Albin Hansson, was arranged—according to Ekblad's testimony—on the evening of September 22 and took place in Ekblad's apartment in Stockholm. Hansson (whom Duckwitz characterized in his diary as a man "who knows exactly what he wants") promised that his government would urge the Germans to permit the safe departure of the Danish Jews and their internment in Sweden. In the meantime, Ekblad was to return to Copenhagen to keep his eye on developments and to inform the Swedish government about the pending date of the action.

On September 24, Duckwitz met with Dr. Riensberg, the German shipping expert in Stockholm. He had known him since the two worked together for the Hamburg-Amerika Line. The two men worked out a secret code that would allow them to communicate with each other about the fate of the Danish Jews once a rescue action would be set in motion. With the help of this code, family members could be contacted and rescuers could be informed as to which transports had successfully crossed the Øresund and how many fugitives had arrived safely in Sweden.

Ekblad's German visa had expired and the application for a new visa might have caught the attention of the security police in the German embassy in Stockholm, who had tagged him as a man with "Western political tendencies and a lover of the Russians"—that is, a suspicious character. Duckwitz solved the problem of Ekblad's reentry to occupied Denmark by an act of sheer impudence. He told the passport control at the ferry in the Copenhagen harbor that Ekblad was a foreign diplomat who was traveling "incognito" on a very important mission for the German government. The functionary who checked the passports returned them without comment and let the two men pass. His face registered a suggestive smile, as if he, himself, had just participated in a historic conspiracy, which he had—without knowing it!

Duckwitz, after his return from Stockholm on September 25, met again with Best. The "specialists" for the deportation of the Jews had arrived en masse in Copenhagen, but the date of the action was still uncertain. Duckwitz immediately relayed to Ekblad the message that "something was up in the air." His diary that evening contains his most forthright condemnation of his superior: "No power in the world can absolve RB [Best] from his heavy burden of guilt and the unforeseeable consequences of his action."

But Duckwitz had not given up hope. The German army, which had executive power during the state of military emergency in Denmark, might refuse to participate in "this dirty business." On September 26, he contacted Paul Kanstein, who had been appointed chief of the civilian administration by the commanding general in Copenhagen.

Duckwitz implored Kanstein to ask the commanding general (von Hanneken) to write a letter of protest to his superior, indicating that the German army could not assist with a police action that would be considered contrary to their "sense of honor." Since the available police force was too small to carry out the action across the country in one night without the help of the army, this might at least delay the action "for the duration." Von Hanneken did, *indeed*, cable his reservations to the General Staff Headquarters, but was refused by his superiors.

His telegram read:

DR. BEST'S TELEGRAM ON AN EARLY SOLUTION TO THE JEWISH PROBLEM IN DENMARK HAS BEEN APPROVED IN PRINCIPLE BY THE FUHRER.

AT BEST'S SUGGESTION, THE DEPORTATION WILL BE CARRIED OUT DURING THE MILITARY STATE OF EMERGENCY.

IT IS NOT YET CLEAR WHETHER POLICE STRENGTH WILL BE ADEQUATE FOR SEIZURE OF THE JEWS AND THEIR FAMILIES—ABOUT 6,000 PERSONS, LIVING MAINLY IN COPENHAGEN. THE OPERATION WILL PLACE A HEAVY BURDEN ON THE ARMY WHICH WILL NOT BE ABLE TO ACT VIGOROUSLY, PARTICULARLY SINCE IT WILL BE NECESSARY IN COPENHAGEN AND ON THE ISLAND OF FYN TO USE NEW RECRUITS. THE BENEFITS OF THE

DEPORTATION STRIKE ME AS DOUBTFUL. NO COOPERA-
TION CAN BE EXPECTED AFTERWARD FROM THE CIVIL
ADMINISTRATION OR FROM THE DANISH POLICE. THE
SUPPLY OF FOOD WILL BE ADVERSELY AFFECTED. THE
"WILLINGNESS TO SUPPLY" OF THE ARMAMENTS INDUS-
TRY WILL BE UNDERMINED. DISTURBANCES REQUIRING
USE OF MILITARY FORCE MUST BE EXPECTED.[9]

Duckwitz relates in his memoirs, written ten years after the event, that Kanstein gave him the "friendly advice" not to undertake any more independent steps aimed at undoing Hitler's orders. He knew about the suspicions of the German security police, who were waiting only for the slightest pretense to "remove" the "untrustworthy" shipping expert from Copenhagen. Duckwitz told him that, on the contrary, he would do anything possible in his power to stop the contemplated action, and that he was aware of the price he might have to pay. "Kanstein parted," noted Duckwitz, "as if he had just said his last good-bye to a cherished child that had been seized by temporary insanity."

On the evening of September 26, 1943, Duckwitz wrote in his diary: "I will assume responsibility for everything I am going to do. I am consoled by my strong faith that good deeds can never be wrong." The next day, September 27, he added: "It is good that Annemarie shares my convictions. There will be no detour from the road I have taken. There are, after all, higher laws. I will submit to them."

The following days were spent with frantic efforts by Duckwitz to secure "legal" exit visas to Sweden for some of the Danish Jews of his acquaintance. At the Swedish embassy in Copenhagen, Ekblad joined his cause and issued a great number of passports for "new" Swedish citizens who were residents of Copenhagen. The archives at Yad Vashem in Jerusalem contain many pages of testimony of grateful Danish Jews who were the beneficiaries of these actions.[10]

Duckwitz had one more ace up his sleeve—the German admiralty in Denmark, which was particularly unenthusiastic about the planned deportation of the Jews. On September 24, 1943, the daily orders of naval headquarters contained the following:

The head of naval warfare reports from "Admiral Denmark" that . . . the plenipotentiary of the Reich has suddenly raised the question of the deportation of Jews from Denmark. For the navy this means the necessity, over a long period, of supplying German crews to the coastal patrol fleet of the Øresund. Minesweeping in the North Sea and off the coast of Jutland, which will be of utmost importance with the advent of the autumn storms, will thus not be carried out on the scale required. Productivity in Danish shipyards will decrease more and more.[11]

On September 26, General Staff Headquarters reported that the military commander in Denmark expressed his agreement with the views of the navy. Meanwhile Duckwitz contacted two of his friends—the German harbor commanders of Copenhagen and Aarhus—who both risked their military careers (and lives) to sabotage the planned deportation. *risked lives*

He writes in his memoirs: "It is a tribute to the German Navy that I succeeded to at least lessen the dreadful consequences of the planned action, since I could no longer prevent it. I reasoned that the police forces would not be able to patrol the Danish coast on land and sea to stop any illegal crossings. The danger that German naval units would have to take over this job was prevented by the German harbor commander of Copenhagen. He saw to it that the coast guard ships were out of action. He took a great personal risk, but he did so without hesitation."

Corvettenkapitän Richard Camman was an old acquaintance of Duckwitz from the days when both had worked for the Hamburg-Amerika Line. As an eighteen-year-old he had volunteered for service in the German Imperial Navy, had been wounded in sea battles during World War I, and had received the Iron Cross for his bravery. His last assignment in that war was as the commander of a minesweeper. During peacetime he became captain of one of the great passenger ships that sailed across the Atlantic from Hamburg to North America.[12]

At age fifty, he was called back to active duty in the German Kriegsmarine (in March 1940) and assigned to the post of harbor-master in Copenhagen (from April 1940 to February 1945). During the last week of September 1943 he saw to it that the patrol ships under his command were "in repair" in dry dock and thus unable to intercept the Danish fishing boats that would bring Jewish refugees to Sweden. The Swedish coast guard that monitored the movements of the German naval forces in the sound from the air and from the sea did not report *any* German patrol boats that interfered with the rescue efforts in the first two weeks of October.

Camman's counterpart in Aarhus was the chief of sea transport, Kapitänleutnant (lieutenant commander) Friedrich Wilhelm Lübke. He, too, had served as a young man in the German Imperial Navy in World War I, had participated in a major naval battle, in the Skagerrak, and had been awarded the Iron Cross. In the last months of that war, he had been a helms mate on a submarine (U-71) and had remained in the Naval Reserves until the outbreak of World War II. He was fifty-five years old when he was assigned to his post in Aarhus in 1942.[13]

He had learned about the planned action against the Jews on his return trip from a brief leave in southern Germany. Shortly after he arrived in Aarhus, he received orders to ready the *Monte Rosa,* a hospital ship, for the deportation of the Jews from Copenhagen. Her captain was a friend of his, Heinrich Bertram, who was stationed in Hamburg. The two agreed to pretend that the engines of the *Monte Rosa* were seriously damaged and that the ship was "out of order." In addition, Lübke informed Danish friends in Aarhus about the planned action. The tug-of-war between General Staff Headquarters and Lübke about the fate of the *Monte Rosa* forced the Germans to procure two new ships from Stettin. They were sent to Copenhagen to pick up an estimated 5,000 Jews for the forced departure to Germany. It was not to be.

A terse entry in the war diary kept by the maritime transport office in Aarhus (in the German Military Archives in Freiburg) and the report from German naval headquarters in Copenhagen (in the Danish National Archives) from the last week of September 1943 note "the interruption of the patrol of the Øresund" . . . and "the flight of numerous military and civilian persons to Sweden as a result of the breakdown of the coast guard service"—with no further comments.[14]

Many years after World War II, a Danish publisher of Jewish descent asked the embassy of the Federal Republic of Germany in Copenhagen to provide him with the orders of the German naval officers that had enabled the flight of the Jews to Sweden. He was informed that no such documents could be found. All participants in this action had avoided written orders that would incriminate them and could be used against them.[15]   *incrimination*

On September 28, Duckwitz was called to Best's office and told that the arrest and deportation of all Jews in Denmark was to take place during the night of October 1–2. The German security police (which was under the direct command of Himmler) had already received orders to carry through the action, and there was nothing he could personally do to prevent it.

Duckwitz immediately contacted his Swedish friend Ekblad and the leaders of the Danish Social Democratic party to tell them about the confirmed date for the action against the Jews. Hans Hedtoft, the chairman of the SDP, who would twice become Danish prime minister after the war, gave an account of what transpired that afternoon in October '43.[16]

He came to see me while I was in a meeting in the worker's old meeting place at 22, Romersgade. "Now the disaster is about to occur," he said. "The whole thing is planned in full detail. Ships are going to anchor in the harbor of Copenhagen. Your poor Jewish fellow countrymen who will be found by the Gestapo will be forcibly transported to the ships and deported to an unknown fate." His face was white with indignation and shame. I frankly admit that—although during those years I was accustomed to get many surprising messages from this man—I became speechless with rage and anxiety. This was too diabolic. I just managed to say, "Thank you for the news," and Duckwitz disappeared. He personally did everything that was possible to save as many human lives as he could.

Hans Hedtoft, one of the leaders of the Danish Social Democratic party. (Photo courtesy of the Royal Library, Copenhagen)

Hans Hedtoft and several of his friends in the Social Democratic party (Vilhelm Buhl, Herman Dedichen, and H. C. Hansen) procured cars—through an illegal connection with the Danish police—and went off in all directions to warn the Jews. Hedtoft himself went to the villa of the president of the Jewish community, Carl Bernard Henriques, an attorney who argued cases at the Danish Supreme Court. He asked to speak in privacy with Henriques and told him: "A great disaster is about to happen. The feared action against the Jews will come about in the following way: In the night between October 1 and 2, the Gestapo is going to seize all Jews in their residences, and then transport them to waiting ships in the harbor. You must immediately notify all Jews who live in the city. Obviously, we are ready to help you with everything you need."

Henriques's reply was different from what Hedtoft had anticipated. He said simply, "You are lying." It took a considerable time before he could be persuaded to believe the message that his visitor had just delivered to him. "I cannot understand that this is true," he repeated

didn't want to spend lives

in desperation. "I have just come from the Ministry of Foreign Affairs where I spoke with undersecretary Svennigsen, who reassured me that he was convinced that nothing was going to happen."

Svennigsen had, indeed, been told by Best that there would be no action against the Jews. Duckwitz knew about that ruse and felt obliged to warn Svennigsen. He could not find him at the Foreign Ministry, but informed his colleague, Frantz Hvass, about the pending action against the Jews. He urged him to refrain, for the present, from any "official" action by his ministry that might endanger the rescue efforts that were to be set in motion "in secret."

Ekblad, meanwhile, told the Swedish ambassador in Copenhagen of the warning he had received from Duckwitz, and von Dardel immediately notified his government in Stockholm.[17] The Swedish government, in turn, asked its ambassador in Berlin to inform the German government of its willingness to receive and intern the Danish Jews in Sweden for the duration of the war. Stockholm was never given the courtesy of an official reply to that offer. The Swedish ambassador was told that this was a German problem and that he should not meddle in internal German affairs.

On September 29, 1943, Georg F. Duckwitz turned thirty-nine. His diary entry that day does not make any reference to his birthday. He writes: "Everything looks dark and hopeless. The preparations for the actions against the Jews are proceeding in great haste. New people have arrived—experts in this tawdry enterprise. They will not find many victims."

That morning, there was an early service in the Jewish synagogue in Copenhagen. It was the day before Rosh Hashanah, the Jewish New Year. Rabbi Marcus Melchior said his morning prayers and then announced to the congregation that the High Holiday services were canceled. He continued:

> I have very important news to tell you. Last night I received word that the Germans plan to raid Jewish homes throughout Copenhagen to arrest all the Danish Jews for shipment to concentration camps. They know that tomorrow is Rosh Hashanah and our families will be home.

Rabbi Marcus Melchior. (Photo courtesy of the Museum of Danish Resistance)

The situation is very serious. We must take action immediately. You must leave the synagogue now and contact all relatives, friends, and neighbors you know are Jewish and tell them what I have told you. You must tell them to pass the word on to everyone they know is Jewish. You must also speak to all your Christian friends and tell them to warn the Jews. You must do this immediately, within the next few minutes, so that two or three hours from now everyone will know what is happening. By nightfall tonight we must all be in hiding.[18]

3

A Matter of Decency

Thirteen-year-old Leo Goldberger was among the eighty people in the Copenhagen synagogue who heard Rabbi Melchior's terse announcement on Wednesday, September 29, 1943. Leo was the son of the chief cantor, Eugene Goldberger. One month earlier, on August 28, the German Gestapo had arrested the chief rabbi of the Jewish community, Max Friediger, and—in their methodical way—had come to collect the second-ranking Jewish official on their list, Leo's father.[1]

They had not succeeded. An upstairs neighbor, a Gentile woman, had told the Germans that the Goldbergers were in the countryside, and the Gestapo left empty-handed. The cantor and his family had escaped to their rented summer home on the coast near Helsingør. By mid-September they returned to their apartment in Copenhagen—the Goldberger children needed to be back in school and Leo's father had to prepare for the High Holiday services.

Now events had taken a more serious turn. But where to hide? The first night the Goldbergers and their four children—ages thirteen, nine, eight, and three—were guests of a wealthy Jewish family who lived on the coast about thirty-five minutes from Copenhagen. But as morning dawned, their hosts had disappeared. They had taken off to Sweden without telling anyone—neither their house guests nor their

Eugene and Helen Goldberger with their sons Leo and Gus. (Photo courtesy of United States Holocaust Memorial Museum, Photo Archives)

German-Jewish maid. Near panic, Leo's father took the train back to Copenhagen to borrow some money and make contacts for passage on a fishing boat. On the train he met a Danish woman who was a member of the Women's League for Peace and Freedom. He confided his plight to her. She promised to take care of everything.

Hours later, she met Cantor Goldberger at the railroad station. Pastor Henry Rasmussen, a Lutheran minister, had provided a loan of 30,000 kroner—enough to pay the fishermen for the transport of six persons. The Goldbergers were given an address in Dragør, on the island of Amager, where they would catch the boat that would take them to Sweden. They first returned to their apartment for a few possessions. Leo's father packed his diploma, his mother—inexplicably—took a bag of socks that needed darning, and Leo took the flashlight that had been given to him for his bar mitzvah. "Then we were off by taxi to our unknown hosts for the night and uncertain destiny," he remembers. "You can imagine the fear in a kid like myself," added his brother Gustav, who was nine at the time.

The father of twelve-year-old Ingrid Nathanson had learned of the planned roundup during the synagogue service as well. He quickly phoned a Danish friend in the seaside village of Hornbæck who offered to take the family in until the trouble was over. The Nathansons traveled north, but their visit was interrupted after two days when they learned that their friends' home was to be commandeered as quarters for a German officer. Their friends quickly found them lodging in the countryside. There they were warmly received. Ingrid remembers the wide-eyed farmwife greeting them with the words "So that's what you look like!". She took them in without a moment's hesitation.[2]   *less fear of consequences if caught?*

For nine-year-old Tove [Bamberger] the train ride that took them out of Copenhagen was filled with conflicting feelings: "I remember, sitting there and being a little scared, but there was also a little bit of excitement for me." After the announcement from the rabbi, her family had left their apartment in the care of a Danish maid. Her father went to the bank and drew out money to pay the fishermen and to buy bracelets for his wife and two daughters. Tove and her sister put on two dresses and a coat and took their toothbrushes. Then they went with their parents to the train station.

> Strangely enough, nobody stopped us. Not the Germans either. . . . We went up from Copenhagen to Snekkersten, which is a place that is closest to Sweden. . . . and there were no Germans on the train to inspect our tickets. . . . And the Germans did not go into our apartment either. They left everything intact. When they asked for us, our maid told them, 'They wouldn't be so stupid to stay home.' And so they left.[3]

When Tove, her parents, and her sister reached Snekkersten, they were met by a Mr. Barker, who took them to his home and told them,

"Just stay with me. I'll take care of you until we find you a fishing boat to Sweden." After some days had passed, they found someone who would be able to take them in broad daylight, at 3 o'clock. "The Germans who were guarding the harbor wouldn't say anything," remembers Tove. "We just walked down from Mr. Barker's house to the harbor. . . . And when we left, he cried and told us he just hoped we would get over to Sweden safely. He was such a wonderful man. . . . He risked his life and he didn't do it just for us. . . . Lots of people went through his house."

Niels Bamberger, Tove's future husband, was fifteen years old when he heard Rabbi Melchior's warning in the synagogue. "We were informed that nobody should go home, because the Germans are going to round us up the night between the first and second of October. . . . We had made some arrangements with some Danish people where we could stay and sleep. . . . So we went to our grocer who was a bachelor and he said, 'Come to my house and I'll take care of you.' He had in his store bread and butter, and milk and eggs, whatever we needed. He took care of us for a week."

The grocer called up someone he knew from the resistance movement and said, "I have six tons of potatoes (a code word for people). Could you come and pick them up?" On the day before Yom Kippur, Niels Bamberger, his parents, two brothers, and a sister were picked up with a taxi and brought to Snekkersten. During the ride, the four children were covered up in a blanket, in case the police might stop them and ask, "What do you have in there?" Then the driver would say, "I have sick children. Just close the door. I have to go to the hospital."

When the Bambergers arrived in Snekkersten, they met hundreds of people who were hidden in homes and basements, waiting to go to Sweden. Somebody from the resistance movement took them down to the pier at night, but the boat they were supposed to go in had already left. Someone else had paid a big sum of money for it. So they had to wait till they had better luck the next day.

Nine-year-old Mette Shayne remembered that September 29 was her father's birthday. He had been in touch with the elders of the Jewish community in Copenhagen and knew about the impending deportation. Each member of her family packed a small suitcase and they slept at their neighbors. The next morning they left by train for the southern part of Denmark, where friends thought there might be a greater possibility for a boat to Sweden than up north.[5]

"There were many wonderful people who helped us along the way, who saved our lives by endangering their own," remembers Mette. "Among them were my father's business associate in the small town we arrived in who took us in. . . . the farmer and his wife who had us overnight on a busy hunting weekend . . . the taxi drivers, whom we hoped we could trust . . . and, of course, the fishermen."

The family was on the farm when the radio news first told of the Danish Jews being rounded up. Mette's mother had all along refused to believe that it was necessary to leave the country, but now she knew there was no alternative. After one night on the farm, they went to a wooded area, hoping a boat would show up, but to no avail. They spent restless hours at a deserted children's camp, shivering in the cold. The next morning they returned to a hotel in a city close by. Then someone showed up saying he had a boat for that night, about seven kilometers outside of town.

"I remember walking down the country road with our suitcases," said Mette. "It must have looked very suspicious. . . . We walked two and two, with maybe a half mile between us. . . . My brother, my mother and I hid on the beach in some bushes, while my father was entrusted with the money that had been collected for those who could not pay the fishermen."

Rabbi Melchior, his wife, and their five children were heading south as well. He wondered whom he would call upon to give refuge to his large family. He also wondered about the holy objects of the synagogue—the scrolls of the Torah, the silver candelabra, the prayer books—where would they be safely hidden? He called his friend Pastor Hans Kildeby, the Lutheran minister at the vicarage of Orslov, sixty miles southwest of Copenhagen. "You must come with your entire family. . . . I can put three rooms at your disposal," insisted Pastor Kildeby. The holy objects were safely hidden.[6]

Later, the Rabbi and his family stopped at the residence of the Lutheran bishop at Nykøbing, on the island of Falster, where Bishop Plum and his wife, within a few days, took care of about one hundred and fifty refugees, providing them with shelter and food. From the east coast of Falster, the Melchiors would embark on a fishing boat, heading for the western tip of the south coast of Sweden.

Throughout the last days of September and the first week of October, the two groups that organized the strongest public demonstrations against the German action were the university and the Lutheran church. The senate of Copenhagen University voted to shut down classes for a week from October 3 to October 10. On October 3, the university of Aarhus also closed. That Sunday a letter of protest was read in all Danish churches. It contained the following statement:

> We understand by freedom of religion the right to exercise our faith in God in such a way that race and religion can never in themselves be reason for depriving a man of his rights, freedom or property. Despite different religious views, we shall therefore struggle to ensure the continued guarantee to our Jewish brothers and sisters of the same freedom we ourselves treasure more than life itself.[7]

Many public institutions opened their doors to provide temporary refuge to Danish Jews, from schools and sanatoriums to municipal hospitals. A special role was played by one of the largest Copenhagen hospitals, Bispebjerg, which rapidly became an assembly center for a large number of refugees. Medical students and doctors who were connected with the underground would alert Jewish residents of the impending danger. One of them was seventeen-year-old Robert Pedersen:

> I went from house to house in the streets of the neighborhood: Skt. Pedersstræde, Vestergade, Studiestræde. Whenever I saw a name plate that indicated a Jewish family, I rang the doorbell and asked to talk to them. Sometimes they did not believe me. But I succeeded in persuading them to pack and come with me to Bispebjerg Hospital which had been turned into a gathering place for Jewish refugees. I merely turned them over to the receptionist. After that the doctors and nurses took care of them. And then I went back to my neighborhood and collected more Jews.[8]

The central figures in this rescue action were a surgeon, Dr. Karl Henry Koester, head nurse Signe Jansen, eye specialist Dr. Stephan Lund, and Professor Richard Ege and his wife Vibeke. All of the hospitals were connected with the central Visitationen office, where patients were distributed to the various hospitals. The office was located in the Kommunehospital, where a doctor was on duty, day and night. From there the Jews were sent to the different hospitals, given fictitious Danish names and diagnoses and then dispersed among the various departments. Ten-year-old Leon Feder, his brother, and his mother were among the "patients." "I realized something was wrong," he remembered, "but I didn't know what it was." He was placed for two days in the pediatric ward at Frederiksberg Hospital before his family was transported north to Snekkersten.[9]

Not once did the Germans penetrate the hospitals, even though one evening Bispebjerg was surrounded by soldiers. On that night, 200 Jews were hidden in the hospital—many of them in the nurses' quarters. It was feared that the Germans would begin their search early the next day. Promptly at nine o'clock in the morning a funeral procession rolled out of the chapel. In the rented cars, which the Germans did not check, were two hundred Jews on their way to Sweden.

On the next day, one hundred Jews were to gather at Blegdams Hospital. They came from many different hideouts around Copenhagen. Each had been told to show up with a small handbag and a bouquet of flowers, as if they were visiting a patient. From the hospital entrance they were directed to the chapel, from which yet another "funeral procession" left shortly thereafter. All in all, the Copenhagen hospitals managed to save about two thousand Jews.

It soon became clear that one of the greatest challenges was to locate the Jews who had left Copenhagen and were staying in hiding places outside of town, but who were unable to organize an escape to Sweden. Most of these Jews were working people without means. The doctors' organization looked for them, rounded them up with ambulances belonging to the Falck Rescue Corps, and arranged their transfer to Sweden. Seventeen-year-old Christian Algren-Petersen, son of a Danish doctor, was in touch with medical professionals and hospitals to find the money needed to pay the fishermen. He remembers:

> They came from everywhere. At home, the telephone never stopped ringing, and my mother had to understand . . . whether the calls were from genuinely sick people, or from Jews who needed, well . . . something else. . . . The reception rooms, the bedrooms, the whole house was full of people waiting until someone had found them a boat. . . . I saw some very moving scenes of people who had to give up enormous suitcases and parcels that they had brought with them. There was not much room on the boats, and priority was not for baggage, but for humans. . . . We had taxis waiting in front of the house, safe taxis, drivers who would not denounce us—and five at a time, every three minutes, a group of Jews accompanied by a non-Jew (like myself) crammed into a taxi to go to the point of embarkation.[10]

Other children learned about the impending deportation in school—from teachers, principals, or fellow students. Nine-year-old Jette Borenhoff was informed by the Catholic nuns in the French school she attended and hidden in the home of Gentile friends.[11] Fourteen-year-old Anita Melchior was warned by her piano teacher, who came to get her. Together with her parents and siblings she was taken in by Danish friends.[12]

Fifteen-year-old Herbert Pundik was warned by his headmaster at the Metropolitan School in north Copenhagen during the middle of a French lesson. "Come out in the hall," the headmaster said and added, "if there are any others among you of Jewish descent, you had better come along. We have been warned that the persecution of the Jews will soon begin. You had better hurry home. The Germans may be here at any moment." In his book entitled *In Denmark It Could Not Happen*, Pundik describes the events that finally led his family to safety: "I ran back to my desk and packed my bag. . . . The boy who shared my desk had just time to hand me his Boy Scout compass as a going away present before I rushed out again. The thing to do was to get home in a hurry."[13]

Pundik's parents and siblings were already fully dressed for the flight when he arrived home. They wore warm winter clothing and had packed a few handbags containing the bare necessities. His father had been warned by a friend who had attended the morning service at the Copenhagen synagogue. His mother had given their apartment key to a neighbor. "On the way down I wanted to say goodbye to the girl on the ground floor, whom I never saw again," remembers the boy. "I still imagine she might have become my first love. But there was no time."

His father got a taxi to pick them up. The Pundik family spent their first night of escape at the home of a business acquaintance in the suburb of Lyngby. Then they continued north in the direction of the coast. Herbert's parents knew a fisherman in Sletten. They had spent summer vacations at his place. A taxi brought them to the fishing village, where they were given shelter. The next day, they sneaked off in predawn twilight to a large white villa sitting on a bluff overlooking the beach.

The house was filled with refugees. Some had found their way on their own; others had been brought there by ambulances from various Copenhagen hospitals. Late in the morning it was the Pundiks' turn. They were told to hide behind the villa by the beach, but the boat sailed past and moored at another landing. The family wandered back to the villa. They felt trapped.

At the same time, an elderly man leaning on a cane went from house to house through all the fishing villages south of Helsingør, knocking at each door and asking for the Pundik family. He was a business acquaintance of Herbert's father. It was late afternoon when he found the family. "My name is Nicolaisen," he said. "I am looking for the Pundik family. Have you seen them at all?" Herbert's father recognized the voice and the family emerged from their hiding place.

That same night, a car with a doctor's emblem arrived. On back roads, the Pundiks were driven to Ålgårde, where they were installed in Nicolaisen's house, opposite an open beach. Nicolaisen found a fisherman who was willing to take them across, and the following night they crept across the road and down to the beach where the fisherman was waiting with a dinghy. His boat was 100 meters further out. Their flight was almost over.

Sixteen-year-old Hanne Kaufmann's escape to safety would take longer! Hanne, born in Frankfurt, Germany, and her family had been on the run once before, in 1933, when Hitler came to power. As a six-year-old she had traveled with her mother, her twin brother, and her older sister by train to Copenhagen, where her grandfather lived. Her father had gone to Palestine. Hanne felt at home in Denmark and had spent ten happy years in her adopted country. Like Herbert Pundik, she loved books and learning—like him she learned about the German plans to deport the Jews in school—during a geography lesson on the morning of September 29.

One of her former classmates came to warn her. "Come, hurry," he said. "There are ships anchored at the Langelinie Quay to deport us. It is only a matter of hours. You have to leave." As Hanne packed her schoolbags the rector told her: "We expect to see you again. There will always be a place for you here. But now you better hurry."

Thus began a flight that lasted ten days—from the eve of Rosh Hashanah to Yom Kippur—a story Hanne Kaufmann later chronicled in her book *Hvrfor er denne nat anderledes end alle andre nætter?* (Why is this night different from any other night?). She wrote it twenty-five years after the event, based on diary entries for the period between September 29 and October 9, 1943.[14]

When Hanne reached her apartment, no one was home. She found her mother and older sister at the corner bakery store. They phoned her twin brother, who was working at a local bank, and then they hastily packed a few belongings. Hanne's sister took a hatbox, filling it with cosmetics, some underwear, a favorite hat, and a pair of smart shoes. Her twin brother took his violin. Hanne packed her schoolbooks and wore her favorite dress under a worn jacket. They gave the key to their apartment to her sister's boyfriend.

Friends of her sister phoned and invited them for an impromptu visit to the countryside. They took the train to Roskilde, wondering if the Gestapo might not notice the mass exodus of the Jews who waited on the platform. On the train were some German soldiers who paid no attention to them. When they left the train in Roskilde, her sister's hatbox opened up and the contents rolled on the floor. Two young German soldiers offered their help. When they had collected all their belongings, the girls thanked them in Danish. The soldiers saluted smartly and left.

The Kaufmanns took a taxi to the Jespersens, who lived in a small house in the countryside. Their hosts prepared a fine meal for them: baked ham, roast potatoes, and apple pie. It was the eve of the Jewish New Year. When Hanne finally fell asleep that night in a stranger's bed, she resolved that she would try her best "not to make things difficult for our hosts and not to burden them with our anxiety."

A test of her resolve came the next morning, September 30. Her mother was not feeling well. She had a severe skin rash and was depressed. They had to find a more secure place, where they could stay for a while, without the danger of someone betraying their whereabouts. Acquaintances of the Jespersens helped with the next step. Hanne and her twin brother would travel to Saxkøbing, where they would stay in a "sanatorium." The inspectors, Poul and Inga Gerner-Nielsen, were prepared to take them in. Her mother was too worn out to travel. She and the older sister would remain with the Jespersens.

The twins went back to the Roskilde station and took the train to Nykøbing, on the island of Falster. There they transferred to a regional train to go to the island of Lolland. When they arrived in Saxkøbing, they were met by a horse-drawn buggy. Outside of town, there was a well-tended row of trees on a street that led to the sanatorium. They were warmly greeted by the wife of the superintendent and given two rooms on the lower floor of the main building—rooms that had large windows and were decorated in cheerful colors. Hanne imagined that she would be happy staying in her room and studying until the war was over.

In the evening at dinner, they met inspector Poul Nielsen (who was active in the resistance movement) and a "helper." They learned then that the sanatorium was a home and sheltered workshop for persons who were physically and mentally handicapped. Afterwards, Hanne read herself to sleep. The second day of their flight had come to an end. On the next day, Friday, October 1, they were allowed to go out into the fields that surrounded the institution. In the afternoon, Hanne was even permitted to play the piano.

On Saturday, October 2, in the evening, Hanne could hear the droning of RAF bombers. They were flying to Germany, the land where she had been born. Hanne felt sorry for the people whose lives would descend into chaos when the deadly load from the planes would fall from the sky. She said a prayer in Danish and in German. There was no news from her mother and sister that day.

Sunday, October 3, brought glorious fall weather and the news of the German roundup of Jews in Copenhagen. "Aunt Inga's" eyes were full of tears, "Uncle Poul's" blazed with anger. But there was good news from her mother. She and her sister were safely ensconced on a farm in Lolland. No one had betrayed them. Hanne and her brother heard for the first time that one of her teachers had made a boat available for them on which they could get a free ride to Sweden.

On Monday, October 4, in the afternoon, they were visited by the local pastor and his wife. The time had come to make a decision. The boat on which they could leave the next day had room only for two more passengers, not four. They would have to go without their mother and their older sister. Pastor Marcussen prayed for Hanne and her brother—that they would make the right decision. Hanne remembered, "He spoke to God as if He was present in the room. . . . For the first time I believed that it was possible to have an encounter with God . . . and could not help but wonder why such goodness and decency was unable to stop evil. I do not dare say yes," she said to her hosts. They learned later that the boat never reached its destination.

On October 5, Hanne and her brother had to leave the institution. Someone had told the Gestapo that there were two strangers in the sanatorium. Their hosts took them to a lane that bordered the fields, and a taxi drove them to their next refuge: a small farm with a thatched roof that was owned by two elderly sisters who were retired nurses. During the next three days Hanne and her brother were not allowed to go outside while it was light. They waited and waited and waited.

On Friday afternoon, October 8, a taxi came to the house. The twins were told to leave immediately—that night a ship would take them to Sweden. Hanne could only take a few of her beloved books—German, Latin, literature, and history. Her brother put some underwear and socks into his violin case. The two nurses waved goodbye as the taxi left. To their surprise, Hanne's mother and older sister were inside. They had lived safely in a cellar on a farm, guarded by a big, friendly shepherd dog whose devotion had put her mother at ease.

They reached their first stop on their final escape route: The residence of the Lutheran bishop in Nykøbing, on Falster—the same bishop who had sheltered Rabbi Melchior and his children. Her mother was led into a small room. "Here you pay for everything," said a sober gentleman. "Do you have the money with you?" It turned out that her mother had some shares in her handbag that amounted to about 6,000 kroner. She handed over everything she owned. The sum that lay on the table was enough to take care of her and her children for two years. At a corner table some ladies handed out packages of sandwiches with buttered bread. . . . Four buttered sandwiches and four tickets for the journey across the Øresund for fifteen hundred kroner apiece. "That was the price for survival," mused Hanne.

More people arrived. Among them were two young families, each with a baby. The children were sleeping. There were rumors that they had been drugged to keep quiet. A few hours later, they were driven to a woodshed in the harbor of Hæsnæs. There were four fishing boats. They would travel to safety on one of them. Hanne was seized by fear when she suddenly saw a man in uniform. But he was a Danish policeman who looked out after the lone mother and her three children. He paid one hundred kroner to the taxi driver for their ride from the bishop's residence to the harbor. Her mother had no more money left.

There was another girl named Hanne on the run who was entirely on her own. She was fourteen when her parents had sent her from their home in Prague in 1939 to work on a farm in Denmark. She was unprepared for the hard work, isolation, and devastating news from home that followed. But she learned to draw on her inner strength.

Hanne Seckel-Drucker remembered:

> One day a Dane came and picked me up . . . a young man from the underground. He said, "We are going hiding." By that time things were already brewing. You knew. There was a lot of sixth sense for these things. . . . I went to the coast on a bike, and we went to a church and stayed in the church for one week. . . . We slept under the pews and they brought some food. . . . I was the only female and the only Jew other than a mother and daughter who were old and pretty feeble.[15]

In the fishing town of Dragør, eight miles south of Copenhagen, lived two women, a fishmonger and a schoolteacher, who became close friends because of a common enterprise: They both rescued Danish Jews.[16] ~~brought ppl tg~~

Mrs. Ellen Nielsen was a widow with six children. To support her family, she had become a fishmonger on the docks of Copenhagen, buying fish directly from the fishermen and hawking them to passersby. She had no interest in politics. A chance encounter with two boys in the first week of October 1943 changed her life. The boys were brothers, flower vendors, in a flower market adjacent to the fish market. Occasionally they had bought fresh fish from her. She, in turn, would sometimes buy flowers from them.

That day, the boys came to her to ask for help. They needed to find a fisherman who would take them to Sweden. This was when Mrs. Nielsen learned that the boys were Jewish, and that the Germans were arresting Danish Jews. "We don't know where to hide," said one of the brothers. Without a moment's hesitation, Mrs. Nielsen closed up her fish stall and took the boys home. During the next days, she found several fishermen who were willing to take them to Sweden.

Word reached the underground of what Mrs. Nielsen had done, and they asked her whether she would be willing to aid more refugees in their escape from the Germans. Mrs. Nielsen agreed. During the following weeks, more than a hundred Jews passed through her home on their way to Sweden. At one time, she had over thirty refugees squeezed into her small house. Her six children fed and cared for them, and her two eldest sons acted as guides, leading them to the fishing boats. After the refugees were safe in Sweden, Mrs. Nielsen continued to hide saboteurs for the underground. In December 1944, she was caught by the Gestapo and sent to a concentration camp.

Working closely with Mrs. Nielsen in hiding Jewish refugees was her neighbor, Elise Schmidt-Petersen, a school teacher. Like Mrs. Nielsen, Miss Petersen had not actively opposed the Germans until they began persecuting the Danish Jews. During the second week of October she received a phone call from a newspaper editor for whom she had worked as a young girl. He was now a leader of the underground.

He asked if he could have tea with her—and if he could bring seven guests. Miss Petersen knew at once that if she answered yes, she would become involved in some kind of underground activity. "Of course you can come," she replied, "and by all means bring your guests." The seven "guests" turned out to be Danish Jews. Among them were a six-month-old girl and two boys, aged eight and ten. Seeing the terror in the eyes of the boys and the baby's mother, Miss Petersen was glad that she could offer them her hospitality.

At midnight a doctor arrived and told the refugees that their boat was ready. He gave each of the three children an injection that made them sleepy. Then there was a knock at the door. A Danish policeman, himself a member of the resistance movement, had come to lead her "guests" to the boat. The three sleepy children were wrapped in blankets and carried down to the harbor.

Miss Petersen's home was tiny—two small rooms and a kitchen—but during the next few weeks she managed to hide over fifty refugees in it—often receiving the overflow from Mrs. Nielsen's house. The underground supplied her with ration cards, but she purchased the food with her own money. Eventually she had to go into hiding herself when her activities were discovered. When she was later asked why she took the trouble to help the Jews, she simply said, "I thought it was my duty."

When the persecutions against Jews began, the Danish police force aligned itself with the underground movement. So did the members of political parties who previously had opposed the resistance movement and its sabotage activities. Many of the Danish Jewish teenagers who were safely brought across to Sweden and later completed their studies in Lund, among them Mogen Adelson, Isak Berkowitz, Hanne

Meyer, and Allan Philip, had received semiofficial warnings from politicians or members of the resistance movement.[17] The political leadership, in fact, had passed into the hands of the Danish Resistance.

But even the underground resistance fighters had a hard time tracking down Emilie Roi's large family, who lived outside of the capital. "While the Jews of Copenhagen were preparing to escape," she wrote, "we were sitting down to a festive dinner table on Rosh Hashanah Day. A Danish friend of Papa's knocked at the door 'What are you doing here?' he cried. . . . 'Haven't you heard of the big ships waiting in the port of Copenhagen to take all the Jews to the camps? You must go out of the house at once. Now!'"[18]

Emilie Roi was seven years old at the time, the youngest of eight children. "I felt fear, but not as a Jew," she recalled. "I suddenly felt we are different." Her family spent the night with a neighbor, leaving their Danish nanny, Miss Petersen, behind. If the Germans hadn't come, she would hang a white sheet in the window. The next morning they approached their house cautiously—and there was the white sheet. They packed some clothes and other necessities and ordered two taxis to take them to the village of Hillerød. "We were so naive," remembers Emilie. "There were a lot of German soldiers in the hotel in which we stayed. . . . I can't explain why they didn't see us."

The next day, her mother and her Danish nanny went out to buy a newspaper. The headline read: "The Germans have rounded up all the Jews in Denmark." Emilie's family thought that of all the Jews they were the only ones left. "When we saw the newspaper," Emilie remembered, "that's the point when the real fear started. Now it was the question: If we are the only ones left, how are we going to save ourselves?"

They left the hotel by nightfall—in a horse-drawn cart, piled high with straw. The children hid in the straw. Their first stop was a farm, owned by the family of their Danish cook. But that family was afraid to take them. So they went on to a friend of their nanny, Miss Petersen, who received them with open arms. She was the mistress of a castle that was already refuge for a Jewish pianist and a Danish nurse whose boyfriend, a member of the underground, had gone to Sweden.

Emilie was enchanted by the castle. "I was sure we had come to Sleeping Beauty's castle and could sleep here for a hundred years. It was so beautiful—just like a fairytale place. It had a magnificent park, and in the middle of it a lake with boats. . . . It had an attic, and in the attic a small, snug room full of children's books. And that's where I spent my days, reading and waiting."

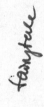

After days of waiting, the lady of the house found a fisherman for her refugees. When the day came to leave, they said good-bye to their hostess and their cook and nanny, and made their way to the fishing village, which was located right near a German army camp. Each of the children was given a bicycle. "I got the smallest," recalled Emilie, "because I was the youngest. I was wearing two dresses, two sweaters, a coat, three pair of socks, a hat, scarf, mittens and sturdy boots. . . . We set out in the morning. Slowly, one by one, we rode our bicycles toward the sea."

4

Escape Across the Øresund

The United States Holocaust Memorial Museum in Washington, D.C., is home to a Danish rescue boat that once brought Jewish refugees to safety across the Øresund. At least three hundred fishing vessels were engaged in the clandestine transport of more than 7,220 Danish Jews and 680 non-Jewish family members to Sweden. They sailed from more than fifty embarkation points along the coast of Zealand, Møen, and Falster, from Gilleleje in the North to Hæsnæs in the South. In the course of October and early November 1943, there were approximately a thousand crossings. The journey for some would last less than an hour; others would spend seventeen to twenty-four hours lost at sea, battling drifting mines and the elements. All told, more than 90 percent of the Jews of Denmark found refuge in Sweden.

A mass flight of this kind occurring all at once could succeed only because it was a spontaneous action of many people of goodwill. One of the main problems facing the rescue organizations was to acquire the money needed for the operation. At first, when transportation was largely arranged on a private basis, the cost ranged from 1,000 to 10,000 kroner per person. This meant that only the affluent could afford to escape. The Danes took it upon themselves to collect money

Side view of a Danish rescue boat, part of a permanent exhibit in the United States Holocaust Memorial Museum, Washington, D.C. (Photo courtesy of United States Holocaust Memorial Museum, Photo Archives)

for poorer Jews. They also succeeded in lowering the price for the journey to about 500 kroner.[1]

Three people played an important part in collecting a small fortune to enable the flight of Jews who could not pay for the journey. Two were students, Elsebeth Kieler and Klaus Ronholt, and the third was Aage Bertelsen, a secondary school teacher from Lyngby, a suburb of Copenhagen.

Elsebeth Kieler, age twenty-five, had two brothers, Jørgen and Flemming, who were medical students and founders of the resistance organization *Holger Danske*. In the course of one weekend—October 3 and 4—Elsebeth and Klaus managed to gather a great deal of money to help the resistance movement smuggle the Jews across the Øresund.[2]

That weekend they went by taxi from one Danish estate to the next. Klaus knew more or less all the people they visited. Or at least they knew his family. Elsebeth recalled that at one place, the Gavnø estate, they arrived in the middle of an evening gala:

Map of escape routes across the Øresund

We made our way to the main building through the kitchen area. From there we came up into the house until we suddenly found ourselves at a large dinner party. "You handle the ladies," Klaus said, and steered toward the parlor where the gentlemen were. It was probably naive of us to drive around and entrust our secret undertakings to all those people. But in a strange way our naivete was our strength. It disarmed people.

"disarmed people"

They managed to collect one million kroner—enough for about one thousand "Jewish" tickets. Elsebeth noted, "It may serve for comparison that after the tour I had two envelopes hidden in my bureau at home. One held the million for the transportation of the Jews, the other held a month's allowance from my parents—twenty kroner for myself."

Aage Bertelsen did the same in his community of Lyngby. He collected enough money to send around seven hundred Jews to Sweden. They all passed through his home during the month of October. In this enterprise, he was helped by the vicar of Lyngby, Pastor Krohn, and the headmaster of his school. They raised the money through subscriptions and funds, private and official, from the non-Jewish administrator of the Mosaic Religious Community, who contributed close to two million kroner, to well-to-do Danish businessmen and the former Danish prime minister, Vilhelm Buhl. The activities of the Lyngby group lasted for a period of one month—until an informer alerted the Gestapo. In November Aage Bertelsen fled to Sweden.[3]

Meanwhile, two girls in Copenhagen—Ebba Lund, age twenty, and her sister, Ulla, nineteen—began to organize a rescue service right in the center of the city. Ebba Lund recalled:

> When the transportation of the Jews began, I . . . wracked my brains for ways to come up with shipping contacts and money. . . . Ulla and I went begging for money, large and small amounts, wherever we could. After a while people would come to our home to donate money. . . . Soon a fisherman and some others became involved. . . . Then about a dozen boats were willing to sail regularly. Some passengers were troublesome, insisting on . . . having large amounts of luggage. Others, who had more of a perspective on things and better nerves were . . . easy to work with.

Later on, Ebba Lund moved her organization to the South Harbor. She became so confident that a couple of times she shipped off refugees from Gammel Strand, right in the center of Copenhagen, at midday. She gathered the Jews at her parents' apartment and, wearing her trademark red beret, took them in small groups to the harbor. "The German soldiers knew what we were doing, but somehow they didn't stop us," she recalled.[4]

Knud Dyby was a Danish policeman and an avid sailor who knew his way around the harbors of Copenhagen. When he learned the news of the impending deportation of the Jews on the evening of October 1, he went to his police commissioner and said, "Please, commissioner, my grandmother died, and I need to take a couple of hours off." Commissioner Bensen, knowing what was going one, said promptly, "Don't you think your grandmother would appreciate that you had one of the police cars?" Knud declined and used the streetcars instead, acting like a tourist guide to a group of Jewish refugees—mostly old people and children. He brought them to a prearranged meeting place in Nordhavn—right in the middle of the Copenhagen harbor.

There he hid them in shacks that were used by the fishermen for their nets and tools, and later on put them on board the waiting fishing boats. "Naturally we had to be on guard not to run into any Gestapo or German soldiers," he remembered, "but fortunately Denmark had a coast guard that was manned by the Danish police force. So being a policeman myself, I could approach colleagues of mine, . . . and every time a German patrol boat would go north, we would send our boats south, and vice versa."[5]

Niels Aage Skov and his friend Thies, members of the Danish underground, organized an escape route that utilized the canals of Copenhagen, which in the Middle Ages had served as part of the town's defense. They obtained a boat sufficiently like the regular canal boats that stop at intervals in the center of the city, where passengers (and tourists) get on and off. They then recruited a retired skipper who was willing to take the boat on a "harbor tour" to Lynettehavnen, a secluded section of the vast Copenhagen harbor complex, where fishermen were willing to take "special passengers," when the need arose.

In *Letter to My Descendants*, Skov describes one of the "pickups" at the canals:

> I stood at the iron railing . . . and watched a family of four arrive and apprehensively sit down some fifty feet away on the bench for wait-ing passengers. The man was clutching a pair of gloves in his hand, our recognition sign. The woman was talking to their two children, bare-ly of school age, who each carried a school bag . . . that held a few necessities. The family looked for all the world to be ordinary citi-zens, waiting for a canal boat as part of the normal daily street scene. Thies was approaching with three more people, and a minute later . . . our boat hove into sight around a bend in the canal. While we watched it approach, Thies came over to me and lit a cigarette. "Last batch," he mumbled. . . . As the boat put into the landing below us, I looked at the people. . . then turned around and spat in the water. That was our signal to indicate that this was the boat they should take. They all trooped down the stone steps to the landing and aboard, the children chattering about the harbor tour they had been told they were taking. A moment later, they were all gone.[6]

Twenty-two-year-old Henny Sinding Sundo and her brother, together with the four-man crew of *Gerda III,* evacuated several hundred Danish Jews from Christianshavn's Canal in Copenhagen to the Swedish coast, right under the nose of the German guards who patrolled the pier at Wilder's Square. *Gerda III* was a nineteen-ton mail boat that belonged to the Lighthouse Department, where Henny's father was the chief. The boat brought provisions to the Drogden lighthouse and had permission to sail as far as the three-mile limit off the Danish coast.

Glory Danmark. (Photo courtesy of the Museum of Danish Resistance)

In the first days of October, *Gerda III* began working as a refugee transport vessel, managed by skipper Tønnesen, engineer "Sparky" Hansen, and the two other members of the crew—"Stef" Steffensen and Andersen. It was the crew's idea in the first place, but Henny's father was glad to have his department involved in assisting the transport of the refugees. He found them a berth that was opposite a warehouse where the refugees could temporarily hide.

Henny remembered:

My task was every evening to look for Jews [that had been hidden by friends and neighbors], to assemble them in groups of twenty or twenty-five, and to guide them to the warehouse, where we hid them. From there they had to cross the quay in the dark to get on the boat. . . . The Jews we brought passed the night in the warehouse granary, watching for favorable moments to cross the quay. In the warehouse we left them something to eat and drink, and also sleeping draughts to make the children sleep, as it was essential that no noise could be heard by the German soldiers patrolling outside.

The boat couldn't lift anchor until seven o'clock in the morning. When it started its engine, the two Germans on duty came on board to check the papers. They never thought to go down to the hold where they would have found our Jewish guests. Every morning, the crew offered a beer to the two soldiers; they toasted each other and talked about the weather. Then the Germans went back on the quay.[7]

After that *Gerda III* took off to the sea. Every day it made a side trip to the Swedish coast where the crew got the refugees safely ashore before setting course for the Drogden Lighthouse. They *never* lost *one* life!

Other important escape routes lay close to Copenhagen. Among them was via Kastrup, where fourteen-year-old Anita Melchior and her three siblings escaped by hiding at the bottom of a fishing boat,[8] and Dragør, a fishing village on the island of Amager. That was the embarkation point for Isak Berkowitz, age fifteen, Jette Borenhoff, age nine, and Allan Philip, sixteen, and his two brothers.[9] Their crossings went without major incidents. October was herring season, when fishing boats were often out in the middle of the night. In October 1943, they transported 600 to 700 Jews from Dragør to Sweden. The local German commander was well known for not noticing Jewish refugees. Rumor has it that he was sent to the Eastern Front for just that reason.

Cantor Goldberger and his family left from there on a bitter-cold night. Thirteen-year-old Leo Goldberger remembered that his three-year-old brother had been given a sleeping pill to keep him quiet. As his family huddled in the bushes along the beach, they were anxiously waiting for a light signal. Finally it came. They were off.

Wading straight into the sea, they walked out about one hundred feet through the icy water, until it reached Leo's chest. His father carried his two small brothers in his arms. His older brother tried valiantly to carry a suitcase, but he finally dropped it in the water. Leo managed to hold on to his precious flashlight. They were hauled aboard a fishing boat and concealed in a cargo area, covered by canvases. "The smell of fish still reminds me of freedom," said his brother Gus, who was nine years old at the time.

As the fishing boat proceeded into the open sea, Cantor Goldberger chanted a quiet prayer from the Psalms. Two hours later, they saw the bright lights of the coast of Sweden. The refugees climbed out of the cargo area and were handed, one by one, into a Swedish boat. "There was a spontaneous hurrah," remembered Leo.[10]

Kirsten Meyer Nielsen, age nine, and her sister Lisa, who was twelve, had stayed three weeks at the home of her father's business associate on Amager after the state of military emergency had been declared. They were picked up on the morning of September 29 and told that they would go to Sweden the next day. Kirsten remembered that her Danish playmates were jealous because they were going to a place where they would get chocolate and chewing gum. When their taxi left the next day, all the children on her street ran after it and shouted "good luck."[11]

In an arranged meeting place, they met the other people who were going to flee with them. Hours late, the fisherman, who was to sail them across to Sweden, came to tell them he had gotten cold feet. He did not dare to sail over in broad daylight. After an animated discussion and the offer of money to help him buy a fish store, he agreed to take them—after sunset. In the meantime they cleared out their suitcases and took only a few necessities in handbags.

They left by taxi to Kongelunden on Amager. On their way they had to pass a large German military camp, but no one approached them. When they reached the beach, they hid in a fisherman's shack and waited for the sun to set. A search light directed them to the side of the beach that was lying in darkness. There they found a small open fishing boat pulled up on the beach. They went on board and quietly rowed away. Some time later, the fisherman tried to jump-start the engine, but nothing happened. The motor was dead.

They went back to the beach, found a boat that was anchored, filled its motor with gasoline, and transferred from one boat to the other. Kirsten's father had qualms about "stealing" the second boat, but the matter was settled by writing a letter to the owner, telling him that they had only "borrowed" it and it would be brought back.

They were finally on the way. It was a cold, dark night and the wind was blowing so hard that the waves swept over the boat. The children and their mother sat in the rear under a tarpaulin, but soon they were completely drenched in seawater. In spite of being wet to her bones, Kirsten remembers being excited, expectant, and happy that the long wait was finally over: "My mother's courage and ability to act in this situation was incredible. She had never hidden the fact that our journey was dangerous. But at the same time, she made it into an exciting and fairy-tale-like experience. The candy was waiting over there."

Suddenly the motor stopped. The fisherman pulled and pulled the starter cable, but nothing happened. They had sailed straight into a pound net; it was stuck to the propeller under the boat. Panic took hold of the refugees when they were not able to get the propeller free of the net. Finally, one of the young men who was in their party went into the water and got it free. The motor started up again, and everybody breathed a sigh of relief.

After some time had passed, the fisherman suddenly shouted that they were in "free water." They had crossed the line that separated Denmark from Sweden. "We were intoxicated with happiness," remembers Kirsten. Even the seasick passengers were singing "We Sailed up the Creek." Soon afterwards, they docked in the harbor of Limhamn, where a police officer greeted them with the words "Welcome to Sweden." Then they were driven in a car to the police station in Malmö, where they were given food, covered in warm blankets, and fell asleep. "I wish that all refugees would be greeted in this manner," said Kirsten. "It was incredible."

Jewish refugees aboard Danish fishing boat bound for Sweden. (Photo courtesy of United States Holocaust Memorial Museum, Photo Archives)

About thirteen hundred Danish Jews left from the small fishing town of Gilleleje, at the northern tip of Zealand. Among them were fifteen-year-old Hanne Meyer and five-year-old Henning Oppenheim.[12] Henning remembered that they sailed in broad daylight at noon on a schooner that had previously sailed with a shipment of coal.

One of the fishermen who helped ferry the refugees across was sixteen-year-old Niels Sørensen, who was working on his father's fishing boat. He remembered:

The local councillors, the doctors, the Protestant Pastors, and many of the villagers came to see if we could help the Jews evacuate to Sweden. It was our mother who told us children that these people . . . were going to be persecuted by the Germans and that they needed our help. It was she who encouraged us to take part in the evacuation. They went down there [through the trap door], and disappeared in the hull. If they squeezed up, it could carry five or six. They could only take one little bag for the journey. . . . Once they were all in the hold, we shut the trapdoor, and we stacked our ropes on top. The Germans who inspected the boat never suspected that under the nets and ropes, there was a trapdoor! We made many trips to Sweden. . . . The crossing would take an hour and a half–two hours, depending on sea conditions.

He added, "When sleeping at home, some of us kept a ladder by the bedroom window to escape if the knock came on the front door." Despite these precautions, Niels's father was arrested and spent the last six months of the war in a concentration camp. Niels himself fled to Sweden, where he worked until the war's end with the Danish Resistance.[13]

Seven-year-old Emilie Roi remembers passing a group of German soldiers who were drinking beer in the harbor of Hornbæck on her way to the fishing boat that was to take them to Sweden. They paid no attention to her and her seven brothers and sisters as they bicycled toward the harbor in their layers of clothing. "Sometimes I think that they just didn't want to see us," she wrote later.

She sat in the dark in the hold, breathing the stink of fish. The boat that carried her large family left at noon. They heard the voice of a Danish policeman on board who called, "Have a good trip!" Then he turned and was gone. As they got out to the open sea, the waves were high, and the boat rose and fell. The fisherman began to sail his vessel up and down the Sund, pulling the net as if he was fishing. He was waiting until it would get dark.

The awful reek of fish got stronger and Emilie ventured up to the deck to get some fresh air. . . . There was a brief scare when a German gunboat passed by, but all the Germans could see was a peaceful fisherman completely taken up with a large net he had cast into the water. Half an hour later, he started his motor and pointed the boat in the direction of the border. He steered it steadily out of the danger zone, where there were underwater mines.

Then they saw a light in the distance. It had been three years since Emilie had seen a light at night—half her young life she had known only blackouts in Denmark. A boat with a blue and yellow flag was coming to meet them. "Welcome to Sweden," said the crew as they entered the harbor of Helsingborg. "I never heard more beautiful words," said Emilie.[14]

Fifteen-year-old Herbert Pundik and his family left from Ålgårde. The last he remembered of Denmark was the faint sound of the boat cutting through the water as the fisherman poled it away from the shore to the open sea. "Looking back," he said, "I saw two persons kneeling on the sand. One was our host, my father's friend, the other was the wife of the fisherman who was going to smuggle us through the German lines from occupied Denmark to neutral Sweden. Their hands were lifted toward heaven. They remained within my sight until the Danish coastline was lost from view."[15]

Once in open water, the fisherman started the motor. Years later, Herbert would still remember the searchlights from the German patrol boats playing over the dark sky and the silent fisherman who was making a dash for the Swedish coast. The boy counted the minutes. From the time they had left Denmark to the moment the fisherman called his family on deck and told them that they were safe, thirty-seven minutes had passed. It seemed like eternity.

A Swedish coastal patrol boat watched the fishing boat from a distance, its position marking the lines of its territorial waters. The moment the Danes crossed the line with their cargo of Jews, the Swedes took over and escorted them to the harbor. After the Pundiks had safely disembarked, the Danish fisherman waved good-bye and turned back to the darkened Danish coast.

South of Helsingør (Elsinore, the seat of Hamlet's castle), is the fishing harbor of Snekkersten. It is located at "a spot" where the Strait of Øresund is very narrow. The first rescue transports from there were improvised and risky. Refugees were sent off in rowboats, sports kayaks, racing sculls, sailboats, and dinghies belonging to local yachtsmen and summer residents. They were often navigated by people who knew very little about the sea.

The local physician, Jørgen Gersfelt, had a special "doctor's license" that allowed him to drive his car at night in spite of the military curfew. He picked up refugees who had been hidden in the summer homes of his friends. In his book *Sådan narrede vi Gestapo* (How we cheated the Gestapo), he related the story of a rowboat crossing: A retired mailman, a seventy-year-old gardener, and a barber helped a fisherman row across the Sund. The currents were strong and the journey lasted all night. The only one with any experience in handling the oars was the fisherman![16]

In the beginning of October 1943, the transports became better organized. Seventeen-year-old Preben Munch-Nielsen was "recruited" by the local police inspector to pick up Jews at the railway station and take them to their night lodgings. The next day, the teenager would escort them from Snekkersten through the woods to nearby Espergærde, where there was a shipping location. "There were so many jobs involved. We had to pick the refugees up at the train station, we brought them to the houses, helped them down to the shore. You cannot afford to be afraid. And if you were, you could not let it have any impact on what you had to do. . . . It was a matter of decency."[17]

One of the local fishermen, Jonas Borgesen, estimated that during the first weekend of October, a thousand people were transferred from Snekkersten to the middle of the Sund, where a Swedish patrol boat would take them over to Sweden. The four-kilometer trip took about 40–50 minutes. During that time, nine other fishing boats were sailing a shuttle service to the Swedish harbors of Raa, Knahaken, and Helsingborg.

Borgesen remembered: "At that time, there appeared to be no risk sailing during the day with the Jews. The route was 300–400 meters north of a German guard ship at anchor, but without any reaction at all from their side."[18] The German crew apparently resented being

[handwritten marginal note:] better organized as time went on

Danish fishermen ferrying a boatload of Jewish refugees to Sweden. (Photo courtesy of United States Holocaust Memorial Museum, Photo Archives)

part of the manhunt initiated by the Gestapo and the SS. Their skipper had often been on duty in Flensburg and Kiel, near the Danish border, and had many Danish acquaintances. He and his crew did nothing to stop the Danish fishing boats.

John Saietz, who was fourteen years old at the time, told of a surprise meeting between his father and a German officer that occurred on the way from the family's rented summerhouse to the Snekkersten harbor:

In order not to call attention to ourselves we arranged that we would walk singly. My father went alone, carrying a small suitcase. When he arrived at our meeting place he told us that on the way he had run into a German officer. Panicking, he had tried to get rid of the suitcase without the officer noticing it. The German told him, "Ruhig, ich tue Ihnen nichts" [Take it easy, I won't harm you].[19]

Why????

Nine-year-old Tove Bamberger went on a fishing boat from the same vicinity. She hid with fourteen people below the deck, among them children who were the same age as she. They had an old aunt along who suddenly remembered that she had forgotten her umbrella and wanted to go home. Tove's father took her leg, pulled her down in the cargo hold, and said, "You are *not* going back home. We are leaving!"[20]

They closed the small square that was the opening to the cargo hold and every one sat around in the dark. When the boat went out into the Sund, everyone became seasick. "I was so proud of myself," remembers Tove. "I was only a child, but I was the only one who was not seasick." After a journey of thirty minutes a large boat approached their fishing vessel. "We were afraid it was Germans because there were soldiers on it . . . and they were dressed just like the Germans."

But it was a Swedish patrol boat that had come to pick them up. They had crossed into Swedish waters. "They helped us from the fishing boat and we stayed on deck. We were safe. . . . We went into a little harbor right outside of Helsingborg and . . . they were welcoming us."[21]

After the successful shuttle runs by the fishing boats on the first weekend in October, the Gestapo intervened. On Monday afternoon, they confiscated seven boats and arrested twelve fishermen as they arrived back in the Snekkersten harbor after transporting Jews to Sweden. In the days after the arrest of the fishermen, it was impossible to manage the stream of refugees with smaller boats. A group of Danes bought a sturdy twenty-ton boat that had been used for collecting boulders on the ocean floor. There was room in the cabin and in the hold for up to one hundred people.

Niels Bamberger, who was fifteen years old at the time, remembered his journey:

The resistance movement had a big schooner—and they took some hundred people aboard. . . . We went out there by row boats. It wasn't far out to the ship and when they had all the people there, we paid them . . . 2,000 kroner a person. That was the going rate and . . . helped those persons who were poor or sick and could not afford the journey. . . . Everybody got out, whether they had money or not. They were all helped to get out. . . . We got aboard the ship and went down below deck and took off. We sailed for an hour or so at midnight, and in the middle of the ocean we had this big Swedish gunboat coming toward us. We all thought it was the Germans. . . . They had the same kind of uniforms, but it was a Swedish boat and they helped us all off [and] on[to] the Swedish ship. We got aboard and they gave us candy and coffee, and then we went to Sweden. We were saved. . . . We came there on the day before Yom Kippur.[22]

Refugees who had gone south to the island of Falster faced a much longer journey across the Sund that would take them close to the German and Polish border. Some endured many fearful hours in crowded, uncomfortable quarters, not knowing whether they would ever reach a Swedish harbor. Ove Nathan and his family would make the passage in nine hours.[23] Rabbi Melchior, his wife, and five children drifted for nineteen hours, and Hanne Seckel's journey would take a night and a day. But they all made it to safety!

Leif Donde was six years old when he fled Copenhagen with his family on October 1, 1943. They boarded a train south and, with a group of twelve other Jews, were taken under the cover of darkness to a beach on the Danish coast. "The only thing you could hear was the noise of a diesel engine from the fishing boat that was approaching," remembers Leif. "My father was a chain smoker of cigars. I said to him, Dad, don't do it, because the airplanes can see us."

It was pitch-dark when the Donde family boarded the fishing vessel, run by three young men who had never sailed a boat but had been given instructions on "how to." The boat was very old and had repeated engine trouble. A German patrol boat caught sight of the party. Since the boat was very shallow, the young men decided to run through the minefields in the water, so that the patrol boat couldn't follow them.

"Fortunately we did not hit any of the mines," remembered Leif. The crossing to Sweden took eleven hours because of the rough waters. Two hours after they arrived at the small Swedish harbor of Trelleborg, their boat sank in the port.[24]

Eight-year-old Mette Shayne was worried about air raids and German patrols. There were twenty-four people onboard a boat made for four, and almost every one was very seasick. "During the night air raids lit the sky, indicating we were dangerously close to Germany, and we began to wonder if the fishermen had lost their way. At one point we were pursued by a German patrol boat, and one can only speculate on how we got away. . . . Did they know and let us go?" When day broke, they sighted the town of Ystad. A Swedish coast guard ship guided them around German ships anchored in the harbor. They were safe.[25]

On Friday night, October 8, 1943—the night before Yom Kippur— three boats put to sea from Hæsnæs harbor. In Rabbi Melchior's boat, there were nineteen people—it was fit for four or five. They left at

Jews on a rescue boat bound for Sweden. (Photo courtesy of United
States Holocaust Memorial Museum, Photo Archives)

7:00 P.M. By daybreak, eleven hours later, they had reached Gedser, a
small town on the southern tip of Falster, whose port was the main
ferry route between Denmark and Germany. Gedser was teeming
with Germans—their skipper had lost his way. It turned out he had
never done any real sailing before.[26]

The rabbi took over the wheel and made sure of a change of
course. After having cruised for a total of nineteen hours, the refugees
reached a small fishermen's village, Lilla Beddings, on the south coast
of Sweden. Shortly before their arrival, their boat had run out of fuel,
but Swedish fishermen rowed out to take the party aboard. They had
never before in their lives seen Jews or refugees, not to mention
Jewish refugees.

Bent Melchior, who was fourteen in 1943, said, "I shall never forget
the moment when after all the hours of fear and suffering a Swedish
fisherman met us with 'Välkomna till Sverige!' (Welcome to
Sweden!)."[27] His father later wrote, "They put us ashore, invited us to

their homes, and displayed a cordiality and kindness which did not fall short of the helpfulness with which we had been sent away from home." Eighteen-year-old Hanne Seckel found herself on a tiny herring boat with twenty-four other passengers. They were sailing for ten hours and still had not reached the Swedish coast. The fisherman had neither map nor compass—he just tried to follow the stars. The boat wound up on the Polish side of the Kattegat. A German patrol came on board.

Hanne remembered, "The German soldiers with their bayonets . . . they were walking on top of the boat. . . . There was herring on top of the tarpaulin and we were under the herrings, covered with straw. . . . To this day, I think that the Germans must have known. . . that we were there." They ordered the fisherman to go back to Denmark. The boat turned around and went in the other direction. Twenty-two hours later they arrived in Sweden. "Suddenly . . . you see the coast. . . . We didn't know if it was the Danish coast, the Swedish coast, the Polish coast, and suddenly we see all of these little rowboats coming out to us . . . and waving. And the Swedes came over in the rowboats and took us in. . . . Now, we didn't even know where we landed . . . and we all just cried and laughed. . . . It was like seeing the Promised Land."[28]

Sixteen-year-old Hanne Kaufmann, together with her twin brother, her older sister, and her mother, left on the last boat from Hæsnæs on the night of October 8–9, shortly before eleven o'clock. With them were two members of the resistance movement, two very old ladies, and two babies. They were so quiet, one might have thought they were dead.

Hanne was hidden below the deck, behind the motor of the fishing boat. As they traveled through the night, heading south, Hanne had plenty to think about: "The fisherman had a permit to fish—who had issued the permits? And what might happen if a German patrol would come on board? Would the men be decent? And suddenly I thought: If Hitler's evil system had not dominated more than half of Europe, there would have never been an opportunity to find out, how decent and selfless people can be."

Suddenly the motor stopped. There was a frightening silence. In what seemed like an eternity the other boat—perhaps a German patrol—passed on. The fishing boat began to move again. Later on, the sound of its motor cut back to avoid a mine, only ten meters away. They had changed course and were now heading north, toward the southern tip of Sweden. Shortly afterward the motor started up again. The mine had drifted away. It was seven minutes before six o'clock in the morning when the motor stopped a third time.

They were across the three-mile border—in Swedish waters. Free! Saved! The broad side of the ship faced the Swedish coast. They came up on deck, looking unkempt and miserable—as if they had been on the run for years. Suddenly, someone began to sing the Danish national anthem: "There is a beautiful country with broad bays and a wide seacoast. With hills and dales, the home of Freia, and its name is Denmark." More and more joined the song and turned their faces to the land that disappeared behind them. And then they sang the Swedish national anthem: "You ancient, you free, you mountainous land, you silent North, filled with friends, with green meadows and rocky beaches, You are the land I cherish most."

The motor had started up again. They were heading for Trelleborg. Despite the early morning hour, the harbor was filled with people, ready to receive the refugees from Denmark. "In this moment," wrote Hanne, "I was offered life. And I accepted it with gratitude. As the gift it always is."[29]

On January 30, 1979, twenty-five years after Hanne Kaufmann had journeyed to safety across the Øresund, the *Jerusalem Post* printed a

letter by Ulrik Plesner, a Danish Jew who had emigrated to Israel and
was living in a communal settlement, Moshav Amidnadav:

> In October 1943, when the Jews of Denmark were being hidden
> in order to keep them from being sent to concentration camps by the
> occupying German forces, my neighbor organized and ran a fishing
> boat service which took groups of Jews across the sea . . . to neutral
> Sweden. . . . On a dark and rough night, my neighbor sailed with
> lights out and the fish-hold full of Danish Jews. He was caught in the
> searchlight of a German Navy patrol boat which ordered him to stop
> and kept him covered. The German captain shouted: "What are you
> carrying?" And Ole shouted back, "Fish." The captain then jumped
> onto the deck, leaving his crew to cover him, and demanded that the
> hatches to the fish-holds be removed. He stared a long time at sever-
> al dozen frightened people looking up at him. Finally, he turned and
> said to Ole, in a loud voice that could be heard by his own crew as
> well: "Ah, fish!" Then he returned to his boat and sailed into the
> night.[30]

5

Refuge in Sweden

On October 2, 1943, Sven Grafström, head of the press office of the Swedish Foreign Ministry, held an afternoon conference with the international press at the Grand Hotel in Stockholm. In the evening, at 7:00 P.M., his announcement was read on the radio:

> For the past few days there have been reports in Sweden stating that measures are being prepared against the Jews in Denmark of the same kind as those previously implemented in Norway and other occupied countries. According to instructions received, the Swedish minister in Berlin informed the German authorities of the serious repercussions that these measures would provoke in Sweden. In addition, the minister extended an offer from the Swedish government to receive all the Danish Jews in Sweden.[1]

For Sweden, the offer to shelter the Danish Jews meant a sharp turn away from the compliant policy toward the German rule in occupied Europe that it had maintained in the past. The occupation of Denmark and Norway in 1940 had isolated Sweden from the West. For three and one-half years, the aim of Swedish foreign policy had been to keep the country out of the war. This had led to a series of pro-German concessions: The transit agreements between 1940 and 1943 had brought two million German soldiers through Sweden to occupied Norway, and Swedish air space and maritime territory were open to the German air force and navy.

The change in Sweden's foreign policy came with the change of the war in favor of the Allies—after the decisive defeat of the German army in the battle of Stalingrad. In the fall of 1942 Swedish public opinion had followed with growing indignation the oppression of the Jews in Norway. The dean of Göteborg Cathedral, Olle Nysted, captured the prevailing sentiment of his countrymen when he said in a sermon: "If we were to stay silent, the stones would cry out." The transit of German troops through Sweden to Norway was abruptly halted in August 1943—a few weeks before the announcement from the Swedish Foreign Ministry offering asylum to the Jews of Denmark.

In the beginning of October there arose a storm of protests from Swedish opinion makers about the deportation of the Danish Jews. The first reports about fleeing Jews could be read in Swedish newspapers on October 3. The papers reported a veritable invasion along the coast from Helsingborg to Ystad—families and single people, infants and old folks, all fleeing an unknown fate.

The same day, the Swedish navy received orders to keep all German warships out of Swedish waters, and fuel was issued to fishermen so that they could take part and collect the refugees as quickly as possible. Later, the local authorities received orders to shield the landing places and ensure that all "illegal traffic," that is, boats bearing Danish Jews, could sail freely. On October 5, the Swedish Foreign Ministry in Stockholm reassured the Swedish ambassador in Copenhagen that there had been no reports of German encroachments in Swedish waters.

Most Swedish newspapers gave full backing to their government's new refugee policy and welcomed the Danish Jews. It seemed that the entire Swedish population was willing to take part in the rescue action. Newspaper articles were filled with eyewitness accounts of the arrival of the refugees:

We are standing on the beach, watching the dark waters. . . . Will anybody cross tonight? Some poor refugees . . . will they escape the hunt taking place on the other side? And suddenly you hear a throbbing from somewhere, the sound of a motor. . . . The bow of a ship appears through the fog. People are crowding the deck, packed like sardines, hanging in clusters over the rails of the ship. Slowly the boat approaches, the pale faces of the passengers are all directed toward the harbor . . . some petrified . . . and some radiant with happiness. But on the faces of all of them you read fatigue, a bottomless feeling of fatigue and resignation. And suddenly the tension is relieved. Someone onboard starts singing "Du gamla Du fria" [the Swedish national anthem]. And everybody joins. . . . They only remember a word here or there of the text, but nevertheless . . . they join in a mighty chorus. It is almost more than you can bear. . . . Here they come, hunted from home and house, driven from their jobs and sometimes torn away from their relatives, and here they come singing as if they were approaching the gates of Paradise. . . . The boat draws alongside the quay. A Swedish officer calls out a hearty "Welcome." The refugees hurry on land with their small bundles. Many fight to keep back their tears. . . . One kneels and kisses the soil of Sweden.[2]

The police commissioner of Helsingborg, Carl Palm, would never forget the first batch of refugees who arrived in his town:

There were about two hundred of them, and among them were dozens of women with babies in their arms. . . . The babies and the children were so still that I was sure they were dead. I couldn't believe it. Why were all the grownups alive and all the children dead? You see, I didn't know at that time that the children had been given injections to make them sleep. I couldn't help myself, I started to cry.[3]

The municipal health officer in Höganäs, H. C. Widding, tells in his diary how he experienced the arrival of the refugees:

I shall not forget the night between the 8th and 9th of October. I had fallen asleep around twelve thirty when the police phoned to inform me that 124 refugees had arrived in the harbor. I quickly got dressed and mobilized the Red Cross people. . . . Among others we received Adolph Meyer, head doctor at a children's hospital in Copenhagen. Meyer had celebrated his 72nd birthday on September 29. . . . In the morning, he received a message from the Medical Association that he had to leave immediately. He was only to bring nightwear and 10,000–15,000 Danish kroner. He had to pay 10,000 for his passage across. . . . Meyer had been hunted like a wild animal. . . . Once he was hiding in a hayloft along with 80 others when the Gestapo came. They searched the stable. . . . They forgot the hayloft. . . . Meyer and several others managed to get away in some cars.

Families were split up, and it was heartrending to hear a mother crying because she could not find her son and two young daughters. I was glad when three days later the three children were delivered to me. I was able to tell them that their parents were already in Höganäs. . . . Many of the children were frightened and did not understand why they had to flee. They were Danish, of course, and had never given it a thought that they were also Jewish.[4]

During the first days of October, before the Swedish government had organized the refugee relief efforts efficiently, much depended on private initiatives, from concerned citizens in port towns on the southern coast to members of the Swedish royal family. A large soiree was arranged in the Stockholm Concert Hall with performances by Swedish artists under the patronage of Princess Ingeborg, sister of Christian X of Denmark and wife of Prince Carl, chairman of the Swedish Red Cross. The event was a major fund raiser on behalf of the Danish refugees.

In Helsingborg, Rose Bertman sheltered and fed dozens of refugees in her own house and persuaded her neighbors to do the same. She convinced one of her friends, Evert Ekblom, to house many Danish Jews in his hotel without charge, and worked tirelessly to raise money

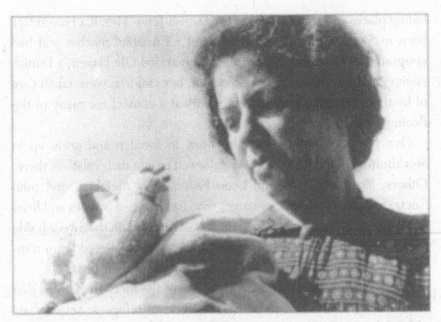

Jewish woman with her baby arriving in Sweden. (Photo courtesy of United States Holocaust Memorial Museum, Photo Archives)

for the refugees and to provide them with ration cards. For her work on behalf of the Danish Jews she would later be awarded the Freedom Medal, one of Denmark's highest honors. Her generous spirit was shared by the people in a small fishing village on the southern tip of Sweden, who received with open hands and hearts a boat full of refugees who had been lost at sea for more than twenty-two hours.

One of the passengers, eighteen-year-old Hanne Seckel, remembered the welcome that was extended to them: "The fishing village had never seen anything like that and they were starting to fight with each other. Now Danish and Swedish are very similar languages. When they get mad, a Dane can understand what the Swedes are talking about, and these fishing wives were fighting about who is going to go to whose house to eat because they had set out big spreads for us."[5]

The Jewish refugees who fled to Sweden included many children—over one thousand youngsters under the age of ten. Among them was Ulf Haxen and his sister, whose mother had been active in the Danish underground, assisting Richard Ege and his wife in finding hiding places and transportation for Danish Jews. Mrs. Ina Haxen was born in Sweden of a Jewish father and a Christian mother and had emigrated to Denmark, where she had married Ole Haxen, a Danish engineer. Upon their arrival in Sweden, her children were taken care of by their maternal grandfather, who was a contact for many of the fleeing Danish Jews.[6]

Ove Nathan's mother was also born in Sweden and grew up in Stockholm. He and his family were allowed to join their relatives there. Others, like Isak Berkowitz, Leon Feder, Anita Melchior, and John Saietz, had aunts, cousins, or sisters who had married Swedes and lived in Malmö or Helsingborg. When their boats arrived on the Swedish side of the Sund, they were met by their relatives, who offered them temporary shelter until they could find apartments of their own.[7]

Others had to spend some time in one of the forty-five camps that were hastily established to house the flood of refugees. Seven-year-old Emilie Roi and her seven brothers and sisters stayed for the first few days at a refugee camp near Ramlosa, not far from the port of Helsingborg. "We met many other Danish Jews there," Emilie remembered, "along with some Danish policemen. They, too, had been forced to flee from the Germans [because of their activities in the underground] and had been smuggled over in the same fishing boats. After a while, most of the refugees moved to the small towns and villages in the neighborhood, from where they could always see the coast of Denmark on the horizon."[8]

Occasionally, there was a conflict between the routines established by the Swedish camp administration and the religious obligations of the Danish refugees who were Orthodox Jews. Niels Bamberger, who was fifteen years old at the time, remembered that they arrived in Sweden on the eve of Yom Kippur and were placed in a big camp that was guarded by Swedish soldiers. They had brought nothing along except for the clothes they wore. Once settled in the camp, their father made the decision that they would attend Yom Kippur services in the morning.[9]

The whole family left the camp on Yom Kippur morning and walked twelve miles to get to the synagogue in Helsingborg. They attended a full day of services, without having had any food. In the

Homesick Danish Jews watch the Danish coastline from neutral Sweden. (Photo courtesy of United States Holocaust Memorial Museum, Photo Archives)

middle of the afternoon, a bus arrived from the camp. All the Danish refugees who were in the synagogue were asked to leave immediately and return to the camp. Niels's father refused to board the bus, saying, "Now that we have been saved from the Germans, we are not going to go on a bus on Yom Kippur."

They waited until the services were over *at sundown*, and then somebody drove them back to the camp. There they were told that they could not stay any longer, because they had not come back with the bus that had been sent to pick them up. So the family walked to the local railroad station, without any belongings and without any Swedish money. A kind stranger bought them tickets to Malmö, where Niels's father had a cousin. They arrived there between two and three o'clock in the morning.

"But we were lucky," said Niels. "We were saved. We were happy. We got an apartment eventually and my parents started a restaurant, because my mother felt if she makes food for other people—she was a very good cook—then there will be always enough for us to eat. And we all got jobs."

On October 16, 1943, the lieutenant governor of the Malmö district informed the Judical Department of the Swedish Foreign Ministry that between October 4 and 16, some 6,670 refugees had reached southern Sweden, 90 to 95 percent of them Jews. By the end of November a total of 7,600 people had arrived.[10]

Preliminary arrangements included lodging, food, clothing, and registration of the refugees, as well as an examination of their papers. After the first few days, the Swedish police were helped by Danish policemen, since both were interested in thorough security checks. They also organized censorship of the refugee's mail to Denmark. Dozens of postcards and letters written by the refugees to friends back in Denmark had to be destroyed, because some refugees wrote not only of their arrival in Sweden, but also thanked those Danes who had helped them to escape. The police commissioner of Malmö explained: "I hated to destroy their mail, but if the Germans had gotten hold of these letters, they would have had the names and addresses of some of the most important underground leaders in Denmark."

Some time passed before the temporary absorption arrangements assumed a fixed form, but the authorities made every effort to alleviate the lot of the refugees. Free medical examinations, and when necessary, free medical treatment was given. The settlement of the Danish Jews required large sums of money that were handled by the Danish Refugee Office, established in Sweden on October 20. The Swedish government placed at its disposal a first loan of 5 million kroner. It increased the sum to 30 million (U.S. $5 million) by the end of the war. (After the war the government waived the repayment of the loans.) The municipality of Stockholm provided a central office for this "state in miniature" that dealt with employment and the establishment of "police authority" and Danish schools.

The refugees tried to establish a normal life of sorts, though, in the beginning of their stay in Sweden, they were plagued by inactivity and anxiety about the fate of family members who had fallen in the hands of the Gestapo. Eight-year-old Mette Shayne's father was lucky. His company was partially owned by a major Swedish corporation. Her family moved to the town that was the headquarters of the company, and her father continued to work in his own company's business.[11]

The first job of the father of nine-year-old Tove Bamberger was in a Swedish chocolate factory. Every day his coworkers would give him extra chocolates to take home to his children. Later he got a job selling artificial teeth. Tove's mother worked in the women's lingerie section of a large department store, and her older sister made pocket money babysitting for Swedish families. Ironically, being a refugee opened up new opportunities for many Jewish women who had not worked outside their homes in their adult lives.[12]

Kirsten Meyer Nielsen remembered that she was nine years old when her mother took a job as a tennis instructor in Malmö. "It was the first time she was allowed to make money, yes, to even be the breadwinner for the family, and she was proud of it," recalled her daughter.[13] Eighteen-year-old Hanne Seckel, who was entirely on her own, took a job in a nursing school in the northern part of Sweden, in exchange for tuition for one term. Then she transferred to another nursing school closer to Stockholm with the same work-study arrangement, remaining there until she earned her certificate. By the end of the war, she was able to get a paying job in a mental hospital. "At the time I was eighteen, I was no more a child," she said.[14]

Jewish singers, actors, and musicians found a benefactor in Karl Gerhardt, a famous Swedish comedian. In addition to contributing large sums of money toward their aid, he arranged for them to work in Swedish cafes and theaters.

Jewish lawyers and clerks found positions in refugee relief work, in the central office in Stockholm and in branch offices, as in Malmö. Kirsten Meyer Nielsen's father held a job as a secretary there. At least 50 percent of the employees of the Danish Refugee Office were Jews, many of them in leading positions. That led to some strained relationships with the non-Jewish refugees from Denmark, who came later and eventually outnumbered the Jews. Most were Danish saboteurs and resistance leaders who had fled to Sweden after they had been discovered by German security forces. Several found it ironic that those whom they had helped to rescue were now heads of refugee camps and on the refugee clearing committees that determined their fate in Sweden.

The Danish Jews even had a religious minister. Rabbi Melchior became a "state-employed" refugee rabbi. In the course of twenty-five days of travel every month, he ministered to the spiritual needs of thousands of Jews who still remained in the camps. He was a rabbi without a synagogue and without a single theological reference book. He performed his job as best he could. "Just as medieval wandering singers were welcome wherever they went not merely because they could sing, but because they brought news of what went on in the world, so I was well received all over Sweden," he wrote in his memoirs.[15]

One of the rabbi's most important tasks was in relaying greetings from person to person, from family to family. In many cases, one Danish Jew did not know the whereabouts and circumstances of another—*whether* he or she was in Sweden, *where* the family had landed, *how* they were doing.

In some of the small and medium-sized towns of Sweden, the communities made their synagogues available for "Danish" services. In places where no synagogues existed at all, Rabbi Melchior was extended offers to use Christian parish halls. After some negotiations, Danish services were eventually held in the synagogues of Stockholm, Malmö, and Göteborg, where the cantor of the synagogue in Copenhagen, Eugene Goldberger, had found employment.

The Danish refugees in Sweden saw as one of their primary tasks the raising of a military force that could actively intervene on behalf of Denmark at the end of the war. In early 1944, they formed what was called a "police battalion." It received its training and equipment from the Swedish government. It later became known as the Danish Brigade. No one knew at the time whether peace would come to Denmark in the way that it eventually did, or whether the Germans would fight in desperation, as they had done in many other places in Europe.

Enrollment in the brigade was on a voluntary basis. About 750 Danish Jews joined. Among them were the fathers of Silja Vainer and of Tove Bamberger—and the mother of Ulf Haxen, Mrs. Ina Haxen. Originally one had to be eighteen years old to be a member of the brigade, but after prolonged negotiations and threats of strikes of the students at the Danish schools in Sweden, the commanding officer of the brigade agreed to disregard the minimum age limit. Herbert Pundik and Isak Berkowitz, age seventeen, were among the youngest members of the brigade. One young Danish Jew, Hugo Hurwitz, chose an extreme path. He returned secretly to Denmark, joined one of the underground groups, and took part in daring acts of sabotage.[16]

In connection with the transport of the Jewish refugees to Sweden, several good illegal routes had been established that became very useful to the resistance movement in the months to come. The intensification of the struggle in Denmark in 1944 meant that it would become necessary to remove resistance members who were too hotly pursued by the Gestapo. They could now be sent by reliable routes to Sweden, where they could stay for a period of time until the worst danger had passed.

Among the refugees transported to Sweden were Danish resistance leaders, ministers, senior officials, officers, and Allied pilots who had bailed out over Denmark. In turn, the routes transported mail, propaganda material, arms, and ammunition from Sweden to the Danish underground. The routes were used as a major courier service between Denmark and Sweden, since Stockholm had become a clearing center for the Danish resistance movement's contacts with the Allies.[17]

Speditoren was one of these illegal route organizations. Established in October 1943, it had brought two thousand people across the Sund by the time the war ended on May 5, 1945. The *Dano-Swedish Refugee Service* was also started in October 1943 and transported another two thousand individuals as well as illegal mail, explosives, and money. The *Danish Auxiliary Service* sailed between Göteborg and Jutland, and this route, too, carried people, mail, ammunition, and sabotage material. The Lisa Route used the regular service to Bornholm (near the Polish border) and passed through the Swedish Falsterbo Channel. Last but not least, the *Students' Intelligence Service*, which had originally been engaged in printing illegal newspapers, established a route in the fall of 1943 that carried couriers, arms, radio equipment, and propaganda material.

During the year 1944, large quantities of arms were brought over from Sweden to Denmark. That included three thousand machine guns, bought in Sweden, for which a Danish firm had advanced the money. They were sent to Denmark in ordinary cargo boats. The arms were packed in fish boxes, which were unloaded in Copenhagen harbor in broad daylight without arousing any suspicion!

Sweden became Denmark's outlet into the free world. In Stockholm, contact was maintained with the Allies. The "cutting office" (Klippekontoret, or K.K.) became a center for information concerning anyone of Danish birth in Sweden, checking credentials to make sure that there was no infiltration of spies and German informers into Sweden. It also took care of the courier service. It employed Danish students, such as Fini Schulsinger, who was a first-year medical student when he had to flee his native Denmark.[18]

Information on events in Denmark, both sabotage and Gestapo actions, was fed quickly to the BBC and the American radio stations in Europe, as well as to the Swedish authorities. The messages to the BBC were especially important because many Danes listened to its broadcasts, and this was the quickest way to disseminate information to the Danish population.

In addition to the transport of mail, propaganda material, and ammunition, the routes across the Øresund brought 40,000 scientific volumes from the free world to the underground movement and to scientific research workers in Denmark. It also brought over 14,000 textbooks and examination papers to students and teachers in the schools for Danish refugees in Sweden.

In several Swedish cities, especially Lund and Göteborg, the Danish refugees formed their own school system (with the help of the Danish embassy and the Swedish government) in which the standard Danish curriculum was taught. The students were mostly Jewish, but there were also sons and daughters of Danish resistance fighters who had been forced to flee to Sweden when conditions became too dangerous for them in Denmark. The schools were run by teachers, headmasters, and principals who were themselves Danish refugees. Among the visiting examiners were noted academics and a lot of "colorful characters." The students took the same examinations as their counterparts in Denmark.

Older students who had been at the University of Copenhagen had their examination papers smuggled back to Denmark to be graded by their professors at the university. In this way, they did not lose any time through interrupted studies. Several Danish students received their law degrees from the University of Copenhagen while they were refugees in Sweden. Those students who preferred transferring to Swedish schools were permitted to do so. Fini Schulsinger continued his medical studies at the University of Stockholm.

Danish refugee children who were of elementary school age (ages six to ten) in the fall of 1943 first attended Swedish schools in the harbor towns in which they had settled and quickly became fluent in Swedish. They uniformly reported that they were welcomed by their Swedish teachers and classmates. Dan Edelsten, who began his schooling at age seven at the Osterport School in Malmö, wrote: "The teachers were nice and considerate and good friends. I had a few Swedish friends in the Swedish school. They were kind to me."[19] Mette Shayne, age nine, adjusted "quickly and easily" to the Swedish school she attended in Ystad. "I became fluent in Swedish, had Swedish friends, and felt no discrimination."

Kirsten Meyer Nielsen, age nine, who attended the Johannesskolen in Malmö found her first days a bit rough: "The Swedish children made a circle around the four or five Danish children. After that it was O.K. and I enjoyed the school a lot. I was quickly accepted by all, so I didn't feel different. . . . I had friends from school and the neighborhood."

Jette Borenhoff, age nine, was also enrolled in the Johannesskolen. She felt fine, became quickly fluent in Swedish, and made friends

Danish Jewish children living in a Swedish children's home. (Photo courtesy of United States Holocaust Memorial Museum, Photo Archives)

with her Swedish classmates, who treated her well.[20] Leon Feder, age ten, spoke Swedish after six months—"with no accent at all"—and adjusted both to the Swedish school in Malmö and to the Danish school in Lund to which he transferred in 1944.

Dan Edelsten, who transferred to Lund in the second grade, found the Danish school to be "an unforgettable positive experience, even though the classrooms were spread out all over the city. We were taught by very qualified teachers (many had a master's degree) in rooms located over a bank near the Cathedral. I learned, among others, many Danish songs, which I still remember half a century later. After I moved to the Danish school, the majority of my friends were Danish."

Tove Bamberger started in the third grade in the Danish school in Lund: "The principal was Danish, and so was our headmaster—Aage Bertelsen—who later wrote the book *October '43*. It was very pleasant.

It was a 20 minute ride with a train from Malmö to Lund. I remember for lunch they had a place where we all would go and eat. It served kosher and non-kosher food. . . . It was a good time for us children." Niels Bamberger concurred. He remembered: "We got the train tickets from Malmö to Lund and some pocket money from the Swedish government. And we were very happy there [in the Danish school]."

John Saietz, age fifteen at the time, transferred from a Swedish high school in Helsingborg to Lund. He stayed with his father's family in an apartment in Malmö and commuted with the Bamberger children to the Danish school in Lund. "Going to school there was a very positive experience," he remembered. "There were many exciting people among both the teachers and students."[21]

In the beginning there was a shortage of books in the upper grades. Anita Melchior, who attended the ninth and tenth grade in Lund remembered that the nineteen students in her class had to share five Latin books. "You had to have Latin if you wanted to attend a Danish gymnasium [high school]," she explained.[22] "Later on we each got a book from Denmark." Despite these limitations, she and fifteen-year-old Hanne Meyer agreed that "the Danish School in Lund was a very good experience."[23] So did Ove Nathan, who transferred from a Stockholm gymnasium to Lund and found *both* schools to be "100 percent positive."[24]

Mogen Adelson, age fourteen at the time, was less sanguine about *his* experience:

I missed my daily milieu. . . . We lived very primitively and scantily. There was plenty of food and it was well prepared, but it was served by some big Swedish matrons from whom it was impossible to get a smile or a friendly remark. The school was very strictly organized. . . . The majority of the gymnasium teachers had very little understanding of the difficult situation that the students were in. The teaching was beneficial, but it was not taken into consideration that some 90% of the students were of Jewish background. It was also disappointing that nothing was being done by the [local] Jewish congregation to contact us. There were some 200 Jewish children in

Students and teachers in a school for Danish refugees in Göteborg, Sweden.
(Photo courtesy of United States Holocaust Memorial Museum, Photo
Archives)

Lund who would have enjoyed a visit or an invitation from the Jewish
congregation.[25]

From the comments of Jewish children and teenagers who attended schools in Sweden, it is apparent that their fluency in the Swedish
language was strongly related to the number of friends they made
among their Swedish classmates. Those who learned the language
quickly reported that they were "very well treated" by their Swedish
peers. Those who learned little or no Swedish had only Danish
friends. Finnish refugee children who attended Swedish schools in
World War II faced a similar challenge. Good language skills in both
their native language and the language of the host country facilitated
their adaptation during their stay in Sweden.[26]

Among the Danish Jewish children were several young girls who
were still haunted by nightmares about their flight from Denmark,
months and even years after the actual event had taken place. Silja
Vainer was only three-and-one-half years old when she and her

brother were separated from their parents during the first week of October 1943. Their parents had left them in the temporary care of a Danish children's home in Copenhagen. After a few days, they were safely rowed across the Øresund by Danish fishermen—in the company of other relatives. But even after she had joined her parents in Sweden, she still had nightmares that German soldiers would come and get her. They persisted into adulthood.[27]

Emilie Roi, age seven, managed to reach Stockholm safely with her parents and her seven older siblings. But she, too, was haunted by bad dreams of the Germans hunting her and her family. "I was running and running, till I woke up, and was so edgy and unquiet that I couldn't get to sleep again at all," she wrote later. The trauma of eluding arrest and fleeing Denmark stayed with her in her nightmares and ended only after she wrote a book about her flight and rescue in midlife.[28]

These experiences were exceptions. The overwhelming majority of the Jewish refugee children from Denmark agreed that the time they spent in Sweden was a period in their lives they looked back at with great pleasure. They remembered the kindness of innumerable people that made them feel at home. Wrote Kirsten Meyer Nielsen, who was nine years old at the time: "My mother and I both shared the feeling that our time as refugees was in many ways a good time. Our little two-room corridor apartment on the fourth floor in Malmö was extremely different from our big house [in a wealthy suburb of Copenhagen], but we loved it because it was ours and it taught us that there were things that were more important in life than possessions."

Nine-year-old Tove Bamberger was grateful that "the Swedes gave us money. They gave us coupons, so we could go into a beautiful restaurant to eat. And they gave us pocket money until we got ourselves established. They were wonderful, the Swedes." Niels Bamberger, age fifteen, remembered: "We were very happy there. We had all the goodies that we didn't have in Denmark—bananas and oranges and chocolate and chewing gum. Sweden kept importing whatever you wanted. They had everything."

Mogen Adelson—who had not been too happy about his school—recalled other experiences that made him feel good: "A very nice touch was that the local women's choir came to sing for us and they brought us coffee and tea. And I had another nice experience: I had borrowed a bicycle and was bicycling to a small town nearby to buy a newspaper. Suddenly a woman came out from her house and gave me a solid pair of ski-socks and a pair of gloves—without any reason, just to keep me warm." And seven-year-old Emilie Roi treasured the big doll and the bright new dress given to her by an elderly Swedish lady who invited her to her home and treated her to tea and cakes on Sunday afternoons.

Dan Edelsten sums up the experience shared by most of the Jewish children who found refuge in Sweden: "All the people we came in contact with were extremely nice and helpful. . . . The Swedes had a very humanitarian attitude. It was the same for people of all social backgrounds."

The hospitality that Sweden extended to the Danish Jews made a powerful impact on the Allies and other neutral nations. In Denmark, there was immense gratitude: Representatives of the Supreme Court, the bishop of Copenhagen, former ministers, politicians, and professors visited the Swedish embassy and expressed their thanks. In the rest of the world, Swedish consulates were flooded with telegrams, letters of thanks, and offers of economic assistance. The president of the World Jewish Congress, Rabbi Stephen Wise, called the rescue of the Danish Jews "a victory for humanity."[29] The *Washington Post* wrote in a lead article, "In taking this stand, Sweden lives up to its own enlightened tradition, but also serves as a spokesman for humanity."

In the fall of 1943, the situation was particularly favorable for such a humanitarian effort.[30] Germany was weakened and had lost its privileged position. Helping a Scandinavian neighbor, Denmark, had the broadest public appeal in Sweden. Finally, the rescue of the Jews was also a part of a goodwill policy of the Swedish Foreign Ministry, which sought to improve relations with the Western Allies and give Sweden a favorable position in the coming peacetime world order. By all accounts, it was carried out with an extraordinary degree of enthusiasm and compassion.

6

Sojourn in Theresienstadt

In the archives of the Museum of Danish Resistance in Copenhagen is a child's drawing of the concentration camp of Theresienstadt, a Czech garrison town located forty miles north of Prague. The drawing shows the barracks, in which most prisoners slept, and the "workshops," in which the able-bodied adults were employed. There are streets named Hauptstrasse, Langestrasse, Parkstrasse, Südstrasse, Wallstrasse, Westgasse, a small park, and the outlines of fortifications and the river Eger that surrounds the town.

One hundred and fifty thousand persons passed through the camp located behind the city walls. Of these around fifteen thousand were children. They came from Austria, Czechoslovakia, Denmark, Germany, Holland, Hungary, and Poland. The artist Friedl Dicker-Brandejsova, a prisoner at Theresienstadt, taught hundreds of these children to draw and paint. Many of the paintings survived; most of the children and their elders were transported east and perished in extermination camps, like Auschwitz. But 90 percent of the Danish Jews survived.

Among the 481 Danes who arrived in Theresienstadt in several batches in October and November 1943 were about 200 former residents of a Jewish Home for the Aged (the Krystalgade Nursing Home) in Copenhagen who had been arrested by the Gestapo in the

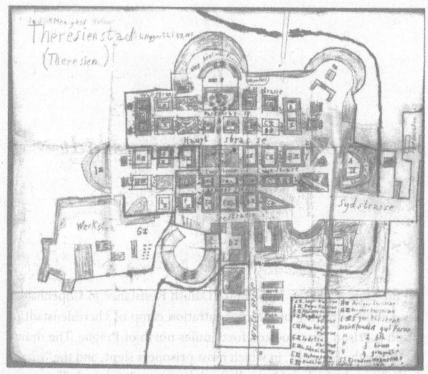

A child's drawing of Theresienstadt Concentration Camp. (Photo courtesy of the Museum of Danish Resistance)

night of October 1–2, 1943. A number of Jews who were living outside of Copenhagen had also been caught. They had not been warned in time to prevent their arrest. Among them were a group of *Haluzim* (pioneers), young Zionists who had come to Denmark for agricultural training, and some children of the Youth Aliyah—refugees from Germany in transit on their way to Palestine. A few immigrants from other parts of Europe had ignored the warnings, believing that a roundup of Jews could not happen in Denmark.

Some of the Jewish families who heeded the warnings were caught while attempting to cross the Øresund. Eighty refugees were surprised by the Gestapo while they were hiding in the loft of a church in the fishing village of Gilleleje, waiting for a boat to carry them to Sweden. They had been betrayed by an informer *(stikker)*, a Danish girl in love with a German soldier.

Attic in the Gilleleje church where the Gestapo caught eighty Jewish refugees. (Photo courtesy of United States Holocaust Memorial Museum, Photo Archives)

On Saturday October 2, 1943, at 12:55 A.M., Police Officer Bouschou heard loud engine noises coming from the direction of the Langelinie Quay in the Copenhagen harbor. He reported to headquarters that the pier was lit up, and that there was a lively traffic of vehicles moving toward the steamer at anchor there.[1] Unbeknownst to the policeman and to the Gestapo, there was another silent observer of the events unfolding in the harbor. The only Danish eyewitness account of the deportation of the Jews was written by a physician,

Hans "Doc" Keiser-Nielsen, a member of the underground, who had tried (unsuccessfully) to sabotage a German battleship that was anchored near the transport vessel *Wartheland* that would bring the Danish Jews to Germany:

> In the early dawn a truck came driving out along the uppermost pier of the Langelinie Quay, moving toward a large ship at the far end of it. And just barely visible out there was a gangplank leading from the pier to the ship. Along this, one small figure after another, hundreds of them, came walking, many of them very slowly, bent over, a few with baby carriages, and disappeared into the ship. . . . Later in the morning . . . some of them could be seen returning by the long gangplank, very slowly. They had apparently been "acquitted" [and] were not allowed to join their relatives. . . . I mingled with some . . . in the yachting harbor. But I could not stay . . . had to quickly go home. It was an evil night.[2]

Johan Grün and his brother Olaf had been arrested by German soldiers while they were on their way from Nivå to a boat that was to bring them to Sweden. Johan described the conditions inside the ship: "It was terrible to see the old people from the nursing home . . . lying there, wailing and crying. An elderly lady, unable to walk, had been placed on a mattress and was lifted onboard by a crane. She was in great pain. . . . If we needed to go to the toilet, we had to climb up a very steep stairway to a foul room guarded by German soldiers who informed us that we were about to sail off to Germany."[3]

Martin Nielsen witnessed the arrival of the Danish Jews in the German harbor of Swinemünde, early the next morning.

> They were of all ages, from infants in their mothers' arms to old, trembling women and old men supporting themselves on two canes. They seemed to represent all walks of life, from young intellectual-looking men to long-bearded Jews wearing peasant coats and skullcaps. One of the first ones to go down the gangplank was a very young woman carrying an infant, hardly more than six months old. The child

was crying and the mother was gently calming it down . . . clasping her precious burden to her breast. The youngest Jews were the first to descend. . . . A couple of half grown boys around 16 and 17 were running up and down the gangway trying as best they could to help and support their relatives. After a while, the Gestapo men with their shouting, shoving and kicking had made the old people completely confused. . . . They simply huddled together like animals in a storm. Then suddenly a group of well-nourished Gestapo officers from the deck threw themselves onto the cluster of people on the gangway, pushing, shoving and kicking the old people down, making them tumble and roll down the plank onto the pier.[4]

On the pier, they had to climb into a row of cattle cars—the young helping the old. Each car held fifty-five to sixty people. There was a bucket with a little water, and another to serve as a toilet. Johan Grün remembered: "On our way through Germany we were aired a few times in the course of a day, so the toilet bucket was not used much in our car. It was mostly used by the children. A little girl . . . who had been terribly frightened by the whole sinister situation wanted to sit only next to me for the duration of the transport."

One of the youngest in the Danish transports was five-year-old Birgit Krasnik, daughter of a tailor who was a member of the synagogue choir in Copenhagen. Her father had missed the Wednesday morning service in which Rabbi Melchior had warned the congregation about the impending raid. Isaac Krasnik, his pregnant wife, and Birgit were among those arrested on October 1, 1943. Birgit remembers the ride on a van from the Rådhuspladsen (Town Hall Square) to the Copenhagen harbor and the bitter wind that whipped around the group as they stood on the dock where the German transport ships waited. She had only a thin jacket on and no bonnet. A ten-year-old girl handed her a hat, blue with red dots, and she felt warmer. She fell asleep to the grinding of the motor as the transport ship pulled out of the harbor. When she awakened, she was in Germany.[5]

Among the "passengers" on the cattle train was teenager Ralph Oppenhejm, son of a publisher in Copenhagen, who had gone into hiding in the summer house of a friend in the coastal town of Rungstæd. There a Danish fisherman agreed to row his family across the Øresund to Sweden. After several hours in a heavy storm, their boat sprang a leak. They were finally picked up by another fishing boat that took them back to Aarhus, in Jutland. The captain of the boat, a Danish Nazi, had wired ahead, and the Oppenhejms were met by Gestapo officers waiting for them at the dock. After the family's unsuccessful suicide attempt and a two weeks' stay in the Horserød Concentration Camp, Ralph and his family were shipped to Theresienstadt. The boy kept a diary during his eighteen-month-stay in the camp. Published in Copenhagen in 1945, *Det skulle så være* (It came to pass) was one of the first Danish eyewitness accounts of life in Theresienstadt.[6]

One of the oldest among the Danes who arrived in Theresienstadt was "Cousin Clara," the wife of a Danish naval officer, who was in her eighties. She had come to Denmark from the Virgin Islands, where her husband had been stationed as part of the Danish fleet before the islands were sold to the United States in 1919. The Gestapo had found her name on the list of donors at the Jewish synagogue. She and her two daughters (in their sixties) were promptly arrested. Undaunted and armed with a hearing trumpet, she became an inspiration to her fellow prisoners who deferred to her as "die Admiralin" (the admiral).[7]

Immediately after their arrival in the camp, Danish Jews were given an "official reception" in the presence of the camp commander and senior SS officers. They were greeted by Professor Paul Epstein, a German-Jewish sociologist, who introduced himself as the head of the "independent Jewish administration." He then led them into the mess hall, where they were served a meal on clean white tablecloths. Along with the meal they were handed sheets of paper and stamped envelopes and told to write home to their friends in Denmark about the warm welcome they had received.

Only after this carefully arranged ceremony had been completed were the Danish Jews "processed" into Theresienstadt. All their belongings, apart from the clothing they were wearing, were taken from them, and for the first time in their lives they had to wear the yellow Star of David. Most prisoners slept, sometimes two or three to a bunk, in men's or women and small children's barracks. Their mattresses, made of straw, were riddled with fleas and lice. Their paper-thin blankets were encrusted with dirt.

Alex Eisenberg, one of the Youth Aliyah children among the prisoners, wrote in his book *Theresienstadt—elegi:* "At night when the entire side of my body is exposed to attacks from holes in the mattress, I fling my hands about frantically to catch the fleas and crush them. But they attack from all sides. First this spot, then all over. Here! There! And everywhere! My body is studded all over with flea bites and reddened swellings that itch and itch."[8]

Birgit Krasnik and her mother were sent to live in a special house for pregnant women and mothers with small children. Birgit's father lived in a separate barracks for men. Like Alex, Birgit remembers the attack of the bedbugs at night as she lay on her lumpy mattress. Her mother would try to pick them off Birgit's face, but it was a losing battle. When mother and daughter fell asleep, more would come. The little girl woke up every morning bitten all over and swollen.[9]

Her playmate was a little Czech girl whose hair became so infested with lice that it was shaved off, making her bald. Birgit felt sorry for the girl and gave her the blue bonnet with the red dots to cover her head. The girl wore it day and night—until she suddenly went away—on a transport to the "East." The word "transport" began to terrify Birgit. It meant that people she knew went on a train and never came back.

Eventually Birgit's legs were covered with a red rash and small pus-filled blisters, and she was unable to walk. She was treated in a makeshift field hospital for impetigo. There she was put in a bed with a Danish boy her age who suffered from the same contagious skin disease—her head at one end of the bed, the boy's at the other. Both had their legs bandaged. After two blood transfusions (from her Aunt Paula) and daily bandaging, Birgit was able to walk again. The little boy who had shared the bed with her also recovered.

The Oppenhejm family and "Cousin Clara" and her two daughters were luckier than the Krasnik family. They were given rooms in special quarters for "prominent" prisoners. The SS officers were impressed by the fact that Ralph's father had published many scientific books by German authors, and that "Cousin Clara" was the widow of a Danish naval officer. Besides, her two daughters were only one-quarter Jewish—Aryan enough to be acceptable.

Their average daily meals were the same as for the rest of the camp inmates: ersatz coffee and a slice of bread for breakfast, potato soup, occasionally containing a sliver of unrecognizable meat for lunch, and potato soup or ersatz coffee for dinner. During the first five months at Theresienstadt, twenty-four Danish prisoners, mostly old people, died from "natural causes"—they succumbed to the ravages of severe malnutrition and infectious diseases.

But the Jews from Denmark who had been deported to Theresienstadt were not forgotten by their government and their countrymen. Barely three weeks after the arrival of the first transport, the Danish chargé d'affaires in Berlin requested permission from the German Foreign Ministry to send parcels to the Danish Jews and to visit the camp. Clerks at the Ministry of Social Welfare in Copenhagen, working under the direction of the ministry's undersecretary H. H. Koch, compiled lists and addresses of deported Jews, which they delivered to Richard Ege and his wife, who had arranged shelter for hundreds of Jewish refugees bound for Sweden. The Eges recruited a group of volunteers and sent them into the houses and apartments of the deported Jews to collect and pack their clothing.

In November 1943, the Germans gave their permission to send clothes and letters to the Danes in Theresienstadt—which was promptly done by the Danish Red Cross. But the German authorities did not yet allow the dispatch of food parcels. Professor Ege, who was an expert in nutrition, promptly convinced several Danish pharmaceutical firms to produce large numbers of multivitamin pills—sufficient for five hundred people per year. The pills were hidden in the clothing. The Danish Jews now had vitamins to spare.

Despite their constant fear and the chronic hunger, some Danish prisoners still managed to celebrate Christmas Eve and the birthday of their queen. On December 25, 1943, Ralph Oppenhejm wrote in his diary:

> *Yesterday afternoon when I left the barracks and returned "home" . . . I saw one of the Holm daughters, sitting at the edge of her bed, her head bowed over a prayer book.*
>
> *She did not hear me come, but sang with a shaky voice, "Silent Night, Holy Night. . . ."Yes, it was Christmas. No one among us had spoken about it—we all tried not to think about it. But it was Christmas; that could not be denied. "Silent night, holy night . . ." and tears ran down the face of Miss Holm. . . .The nurse from our block came and told us that at six o'clock there would be a church service in the camp. Miss Holm took her coat and asked me if I would come along, so we both went to the Christmas service. . . . Snow fell through the leaky roof and covered the faces of the people who had assembled. The room was filled to the rafters.There was an altar—a bed stand, covered with a brown blanket. And on it was a huge primitive picture of Mary with her child, drawn with a pencil.We sang a few carols, and then the Protestant minister, a small red-nosed man from Hamburg, read the Gospel and preached on the theme, "Love your enemies, bless those who curse you, be kind to those who hate you, pray for those who persecute you."His wife and son have been sent away with the last transport, but he can still speak with authority—I cannot do that.*
>
> *My mother asked the Holms to join us in our room. . . . She had decorated it with the light of a candle, the only one we had brought from home. Everyone came with his slice of bread. The school teacher banged his spoon against his battered canteen, rose, and gave a very fine speech about the King. Then we made several toasts with our tin cups of ersatz coffee, first in honor of the King, then in honor of the Queen whose birthday was on Christmas Eve, and then . . . in remembrance of "absent friends.". . . In spite of our rags, and of the vermin and dirt that surrounded us, we kept our decorum. Around seven thirty, there was a knock at our door. Our visitor, Jacobsen, owner of a large estate in Denmark, was a sorry sight. . . . He sat down and complained immediately about*

being hungry. . . . My mother still had some bread. . . . He looked at it
for a long time, like a dog pleading for a morsel, and she gave it to him.

Slowly his sadness vanished, and he suggested that we might invite
each other to a sumptuous supper. His menu included bouillon, arti-
chokes, smoked salmon, roast beef, roast goose, and pineapple. Mother, in
turn, served salmon, green asparagus, roast duck, and a cream torte with
ice. . . . Father's menu included bouillon, smoked tongues with olives,
roast lamb with peas, and caramel pudding. The wife of the admiral
imagined a dinner that she had eaten in her parents' house in St.
Thomas: Turtle soup, rice with curry, sausages, fried bananas and fruit
salad. . . . I still remember the simple home-spun meal of the school
teacher: Pea soup, roast goose, pancakes. After that, none of us could
sleep, and we stayed awake most of the night and talked.[10]

In the waning days of 1943 the Danish legation in Berlin continued
to press the German Foreign Ministry for the release of half-Jews.
They were assured that "each case will be thoroughly investigated,
and only when it is clear beyond a shadow of doubt that an error has
occurred will the deportees be returned." By mid-January 1944,
"Cousin Clara's" two daughters and three other half-Aryan prisoners
were allowed to go home. Ralph Oppenhejm wrote in his diary:

January 13, 1944

Yesterday the two Miss Holms were suddenly ordered to appear with-
in a quarter of an hour at the commander's office. Their father was
Aryan, they had been baptized—they could go home. Their mother had
to stay. No discussions. It was an order.

The joyous anticipation of a return to Denmark turned to sorrow. It
was moving to see how brave the wife of the admiral behaved; she would
have to separate from her children, perhaps never to see them again. The
daughters were totally debilitated in their despair, but their mother, in
tears, packed their belongings and put their bread and sugar rations in
their small suitcase. The daughters took it out—what should they do
with the bread?—but their mother put it back in again. "One never

knows how long you are going to be on the journey," she said. "I know I
will get some more."

We went into our room, to leave them alone for a few last minutes.
Before they departed, they came to see us and say goodbye. They looked
as if they had been sentenced to death. Now they are gone—on the way
to Denmark. I am convinced that they will arrive safely at home. Perhaps
they will tell people about our situation and will see to it that we will
receive some packages with food. But the old lady is anxious about their
fate. She does not sleep, she does not eat, and she cries all the time.[11]

Having outwitted the Germans before, Professor Ege now sought
to get around the German ban on food packages. He had learned that
personal mail (which had been permitted by the German authorities
since November 1943) reached the prisoners in Theresienstadt, even
if it was originally sent to the old addresses in Denmark. German
postal workers handled this mail as they would other personal mail,
tracing the whereabouts of the Jews and eventually delivering it to
the recipients in the camps. This raised an intriguing question: If the
German postal system handled prisoner mail as conscientiously as it
would regular civilian mail, could it be used to deliver food parcels as
well? He and his fellow Danes decided to test this hypothesis.

In January 1944, Ege recruited forty Danish clergymen, gave each
the names of ten Jewish prisoners from his card index, and asked
them to send food parcels to individual prisoners. The plan worked.
The first food parcels reached Theresienstadt in February. From then
on, the clergymen in Denmark were sending as many as seven hundred food parcels a month to Theresienstadt, and the German postal
authorities dutifully delivered them.

The clergymen requested return receipts for each parcel sent and
usually received proof of delivery within nine days of mailing. The
receipt was acknowledged by special cards on which the Danes succeeded, by hints incomprehensible to the German camp authorities,
to communicate the need for more food. Many sent their regards to
a well-known grocer or a sausage factory in Copenhagen. For some,
like Birgit's little brother Preben, who was born in February 1944,

the packages with powdered milk and food sustained a fragile new life. For others, they came too late. Wrote Ralph Oppenhejm on March 3, 1944: "Jacobsen died yesterday. . . . Yesterday, when I visited him the last time, he had just received his first food package from Denmark. . . . He suffered from serious dysentery and was not allowed to eat anything. Now he is dead."[12]

In May 1944, six months after the Danish Foreign Ministry and the Danish Red Cross had first requested permission to visit the Danish Jews in Theresienstadt, Himmler finally gave permission for the visit, and the date was fixed for June 23, 1944. Meanwhile, the Germans embarked on a massive "beautification" of the entire town so that it could be presented to the visitors as a model camp. The German word "Stadtverschönerung" seemed preferable to the dreaded word "Transport," and scores of Jewish prisoners set about to clean streets, paint buildings, and plant rosebushes.

They carefully laid out a playground for children and built a pavilion of wood and glass, decorated on the outside with pictures of animals, and containing inside a kitchen, beds, and brand-new play equipment. Behind the pavilion was a small park, with a children's playground, a wading pool, sandboxes, and a large collection of toys. Birgit Krasnik would play there on the day of the visit. In a nearby schoolhouse, there was a *Kinderkrippe,* a room for small toddlers, with new furniture and toys.

In order to relieve the congestion of Theresienstadt, around three thousand recent arrivals, mostly Dutch Jews, were shipped to Auschwitz, where they would eventually die in the gas chambers. Most of the Danish prisoners, however, were moved into better living quarters. Houses that were destined for inspection were cleaned and painted; the rooms on the ground floors, where the inspection team would be led, were properly furnished, and decorated with potted plants and colorful prints. In the new "homes" of the Danes, some members of each household were hidden in more crowded upstairs quarters, so as to give the illusion of spaciousness in the downstairs rooms. On the day of the visit, invalids and cripples were banned from the street, and people were encouraged to wear their best clothes.

When the long-awaited day of the commission's visit arrived, the weather was beautiful. The visitors were two Danes, Frantz Hvass, from the Danish Foreign Ministry, and Dr. Juel Henningsen, from the Danish Ministry of Health. The third observer, a Swiss, Dr. Rosell, came as a representative of the International Red Cross. They were greeted by Dr. Paul Epstein, who informed them about the structure and administration of the "Jewish Settlement Area" and then carefully guided them over a preselected path—past the park, past the children's pavilion, and eventually into the living quarters of the Danes—always in the company of German officials.

Here is Ralph Oppenhejm's account of the visit:

June 23, 1944

> *Today was the big day. . . . Perhaps the visitors have understood and will tell the world the truth—a part of the truth. Although the old and sick were forbidden to show up on the streets, these men . . . must have noticed how miserable and sick the people [in the camp] look and how slowly they move. . . .*
>
> *In the kindergarten, the children ate bread with sardines and were told to greet the camp commander, "Good morning, Uncle Rahm, come play with us.". . . In the "Park" surrounding the "Kinderpavillion" there was a row of prams with the healthiest-looking children (i.e. the most recent arrivals). When the commission arrived, they were taken out of their carriages by special "nurses.". . . One of the members of the commission asked why everything looked so new. "Things have just been renovated," answered Epstein.*
>
> *"They were deeply moved when they saw us wearing the yellow star," reported my father. "The way they pressed my hand when they arrived and when they left—I could sense that they understood everything. I am quite sure. . . . The man from the foreign ministry held back and whispered a greeting from the King."[3]*

Rabbi Friediger, the spiritual leader of the Danish Jews in Theresienstadt, later wrote: "It is impossible for me to describe the feeling which penetrated my heart in that moment . . . when these words were said to me, *"The King sends his best regards."!* Was it not a blessed country where a king sends regards to a Jew?" And as Dr. Hvass and Dr. Henningsen passed among the Danish Jews to shake their hands, a fellow prisoner remarked to the rabbi: "It is now that I feel redeemed as a human being in my own eyes. Once again I have a certain value as a man. These Danes have given it back to me."[14]

Eyewitness reports confirm that the Danish Jews—following German orders relayed to them by Dr. Epstein on the day before the visit—uttered no complaints about the conditions in the camp. They *did* request that more food parcels should be sent and that books be added. From the German point of view, the inspection had been a success.

Within a month, the three visitors submitted three independent reports to the International Red Cross and the Danish government. Each report mentioned that the town was clean, the people they saw looked healthy and wore tidy clothes—"even better than the normal dress of the Germans at the time." Sanitary and health arrangements were satisfactory, and housing conditions were cramped, but bearable. Of the three Dr. Henningsen, from the Danish Ministry of Health, seemed more skeptical than the other two.

After the war, Dr. Hvass explained to a critical Danish parliamentary commission:

> Dr. Henningsen and myself were naturally aware that many of the arrangements we saw in Theresienstadt had been made solely in connection with our visit. What we paid particular attention to, however, was not these measures, but the state of health of the Danish Jews, their clothing and their housing conditions . . . that could by no means be compared with those of their coreligionists who lived in the real concentration camps.[15]

For the Danish Jews the visit produced lasting improvements. The dispatch of food parcels was now officially permitted and was thereafter organized by the Red Cross. Even Danish Jews, like Silja Vainer's family, who had fled to Sweden, could now send food, including precious lemons, to their relatives in the camp.[16] Birgit Krasnik remembers fondly the biscuit she received from an aunt on her sixth birthday.

The internees also received a large consignment of books as requested, and since there was no formal education for the children in Theresienstadt, curious youth, like Ralph Oppenhejm, could enjoy their favorite pastime—reading. The children's pavilion and the toys with which Birgit Krasnik had played on the day of the visit were locked up. Henceforth she and the other children could only look at them behind barred windows. But the food rations her family received remained larger. The Danes who had been moved into showcase quarters for the visit were permitted to remain in them.

For a while, they were filled with a spirit of "hectic optimism," according to one of the Zionist youth leaders, Ze'ev Shek. He wrote about his feelings after the war: "The optimism, exaggerated and mistaken though it may have been . . . stimulated the spirit of resistance, and strengthened the will to live—and thanks to this the people held out. . . . Self-confidence and faith in the final collapse of the Germans grew—at least among the young."[17]

Even among older people, where depression was still widespread, there was an encouraging sign: After the arrival of the food packages and until Liberation, only twenty-seven more perished, that is, the mortality rate dropped by 50 percent.

The food and the privileged material situation of the Danish Jews earned for them a special status in the camp and, on occasion, jealousy. The goods they received were in great demand by Jewish prisoners from other countries and could also be used as a means of bribery with the German and Czech staff of the camp. The teenager Ralph Oppenhejm writes with indignation about the "many fourteen- and fifteen-year-old girls who sell their bodies for a few potatoes or a slice of bread" and notes that "the Danes are highly valued because of their packages, and a girl is almost as highly regarded if she can catch a Dane as if she succeeds in getting engaged to a cook."[18]

The visit by the commission had taken place two and one-half weeks after D Day—the Allied landing at Normandy beach in France. Everyone sensed that Germany was losing the war. During the summer and fall, the prisoners at Theresienstadt were inundated with false rumors about the progress of the invasion—mostly overheard from the conversations of Czech guards stationed in the camp.

But the euphoria among the Danish Jews soon subsided. Hope among prisoners of all nationalities in the camp faded in the fall of 1944 as new transports carried thirteen thousand Jews from Theresienstadt to their death in the extermination camps in the East. There were seven transports in the month of October 1944 alone. The last reached Auschwitz by October 30. But the Germans had "officially" exempted all Danish Jews from the evacuation trains that rolled to the killing centers in the East.

In the fall and winter of 1944, Dr. Hvass, from the Danish Foreign Ministry, began a series of diplomatic negotiations with various German authorities in order to obtain the early release of prisoners who had not engaged in "acts of war." Even Reichsbevollmächtiger Werner Best agreed with his argument that the Danish Jews had not been involved in acts of sabotage or espionage before they were interned in Theresienstadt. An unlikely mediator that finally made it possible to achieve such a release was Felix Kersten—a controversial figure who was adept (literally and figuratively) at manipulating his most famous client—SS Chief Heinrich Himmler, the man in charge of the "Final Solution."[19]

Kersten had been educated in Berlin as a physical therapist and had become Himmler's masseur prior to the outbreak of World War II. During the war he carried a Finnish passport. As the conflict progressed, he established his home in neutral Sweden and commuted from Stockholm to Berlin to care for his patient. Swedish and British diplomats thought he was tainted by his association with Himmler. But he apparently did not share Himmler's extreme political beliefs and had repeatedly tried to use Himmler's dependence on his treatment to aid various individuals who ran afoul of the "justice" of the Third Reich, including many Jews.

Count Folke Bernadotte, of the Swedish Red Cross, who succeeded in the rescue of all Scandinavian prisoners in Germany. (Photo courtesy of the Museum of Danish Resistance 1940–1945. Photographer: Mosens Amanes)

Better known than Kersten was Count Folke Bernadotte, a nephew of the Swedish king and vice president of the Swedish Red Cross. On February 12, 1945, he received formal instructions from the chairman of the Red Cross, Prince Carl, to fly to Berlin to negotiate with the Germans the rescue and transfer of Scandinavian prisoners to Sweden.[20] Felix Kersten smoothed the way for Bernadotte to meet with Himmler—at a time when the Allied forces had already crossed the German borders, and when the major German cities had been reduced to rubble as a result of saturation bombing by British and American planes.

Himmler's concessions came slowly. Only when the Allied armies were approaching the "collection center" for the Scandinavians at Neuengamme, near Hamburg, did he agree to their transfer to Sweden "for the duration of the war." By then it was April 9, 1945— five years to the day when Denmark and Norway had been occupied by the Germans. And finally, on April 12, thirty-five white buses, with the Red Cross and the Swedish flag painted on each side, began their four-day journey to Theresienstadt. It was a dangerous journey for the big buses, driving on the German main roads. Allied pilots could easily mistake them for German troop movements, and indeed, some of the vehicles were damaged by Allied planes.

That same day, Ralph Oppenhejm wrote in his Theresienstadt diary: "The school teacher is dead. . . . I grieve about all who have died here, especially about him who had struggled so courageously, with the hope to get home to Denmark—even for only half an hour. And now, he has to die, now toward the end."[21]

On Friday, April 13, Dr. Johannes Holm, a medical officer of the Danish legation in Berlin, arrived at camp headquarters. Before he left Denmark, Holm had filled up his car with Danish delicacies—sausage, beer, schnapps, butter, pastries—and had thrown a party for Dr. Rennau, the German officer who was the liaison with Bernadotte's headquarters. . . . After many hours of drinking and eating, Dr. Holm convinced the officer to sign a piece of paper that authorized the release of the Danish Jews from the Theresienstadt Concentration Camp. A little Danish *snaps* had gone a long way to assure the freedom of the prisoners!

Liberation came as a complete surprise to the Danish Jews. Rabbi Friediger recalled later: "At eleven o'clock [on Friday, April 13], a Czech girl burst into my room and cried 'There is a Danish car in front of headquarters.' I thought she was making fun of me. You see, I had told her several times that I had dreamt of our return home and that they would come to fetch us . . . with thirty or forty buses from Copenhagen."[22]

The Danes were told to pack their belongings. A few hours after that announcement, Friediger walked through the Danish quarters and found a family with two children, sitting in tears, incapable of packing. Everyone assembled that evening in one of the barracks; the white buses arrived the next night. The last entry in Ralph Oppenhejm's diary reads:

April 14, 1945

Is it true—O Lord, is it really true? We can leave—we will be free—we will be human again. We shall go back to life, we shall live. . . . I will never forget the 13th of April—yesterday. . . . In the afternoon . . . a door flung open and Mrs. Hald entered, white-faced, shivering all over her body, "We are being sent to Sweden! We are being sent to Sweden!" Tears were streaming down her cheeks. . . . Then she dis- appeared.

Mademoiselle, a French prisoner, asked "Qu'est-ce qu'elle dit?" [What is she saying?] I told her the news. She embraced me, "I congrat- ulate you. . . . How wonderful for you." I did not know how to reply, I was too overwhelmed by the pure and selfless joy that resonated in her voice. It is unbelievable that she could talk that way when she saw how someone else would be released into freedom, and when she knew that she herself would remain imprisoned. When we opened the door, we saw men, women and children . . . weeping and laughing . . . embracing each other.

Now we sit here, waiting to be transported north. The journey will be on buses provided by the Swedish Red Cross. Some are anxious about the journey through Germany . . . but I am sure that all will go well. The fact is that we will leave . . . this black, suffocating, poisonous tun- nel and we shall see the light of the day. I feel as if my soul had been blinded, and now I have suddenly regained my eyesight.[23]

One of the children, Birgit Krasnik, was afraid of the journey. In the evening before their departure, her father had shown her the white buses with the Red Cross that had lined up in the streets of Theresienstadt. He had put on his blue headcovering that he used to wear when he went to the synagogue in Copenhagen, and he told her that the buses would take them home to Denmark. Birgit remembers that she began to cry and became sick to her stomach. She felt certain that it was just another "transport" that would take them to another bad place.

On Sunday, April 15, 425 Danish Jews were loaded on the convoy of white buses. Fifty-three had died in the camp. On their way through the ghetto, the remaining prisoners lined the sides of the streets and waved their good-byes. The camp commander, Rahm, gave an order for a band to play in the central square. "We approached the gate of the ghetto," wrote Rabbi Friediger later. "The gate was opened—and we were free men. No one said a word."

The Swedes had to maneuver their buses between the Russian and American front lines. They passed through gutted Dresden, where Allied bombers had unleashed a deadly firestorm. The buses continued to make their way north through an utterly destroyed land.

They passed through Potsdam, north of Berlin, where ruins still burned after the raids of the previous night. Huge beams of light crisscrossed the sky, searching for Allied planes that were continuing to rain down bombs. The convoy pulled to the side of the road, and everyone scrambled off the buses, seeking the shelter of the nearby woods. The driver of the bus that transported Birgit and her family had fallen asleep on the wheel and driven into a light pole. They were transferred to another bus. In all the tumult, they almost forgot her fourteen-month-old baby brother, whom they had placed in the baggage net. He was barely conscious and was hurriedly given a drink of water to revive him.

Two days after they had left Theresienstadt, the convoy crossed the Danish border. Thousands of Danes stood in the streets, waving Danish flags, cheering the prisoners, bringing them cigarettes, flowers, sandwiches, and sweets. The convoy passed through the island of Funen, and on to the free port of Copenhagen (Frihavn). Ferries carried the buses to Malmö, where Rabbi Marcus Melchior welcomed them.[24]

In Sweden, the Danish Jews were held in quarantine for some weeks. A measles epidemic had broken out, and most of the children in the convoy, including Birgit, became seriously ill. But this time, their stay "in camp" was short. On May 4, 1945, the German forces in Denmark surrendered. The Krasniks, the Oppenhejms, and "Cousin Clara" returned home—survivors of a sojourn to the brink

Danes welcome Jews returning from Theresienstadt on the white buses of the Swedish Red Cross. (Photo courtesy of the Museum of Danish Resistance)

of death. "If I hadn't been so mad at those Nazis," said eighty-three-year-old Clara at the end of the war, "I would have died a long time ago." She came back to her beloved Denmark, herself and her hearing trumpet intact.

The remaining inhabitants of Theresienstadt survived as well. On April 29, one day before Hitler committed suicide in his bunker in Berlin, a Swiss representative of the International Red Cross, Monsieur Dunant, took the town under his protection. Eventually it would come under Czech control and be known by its Czech name, Terezin. In the months to come it would fill up with other prisoners, many of them children and teenagers. They, too, would be ill-housed, poorly nourished, and clothed in rags. They were German refugees. History had come full circle.[25]

7

Turmoil in Copenhagen

On a March afternoon, in her sunny apartment in the Borgmester Jensens Allee, Hanne Schulsinger told me the story of how she and her mother managed to stay in Copenhagen while the rest of her family escaped to Sweden. The story is a tribute to Hanne's courage and the decency of many "ordinary" Danes who chose not to betray a young Jewish girl who was hiding from the Gestapo. Unlike the story of Anne Frank, Hanne's tale has a happy ending:

> When the Germans occupied us, I was thirteen years old. My father had always been politically active in the Jewish community. He came from Poland to Denmark when he was in his early twenties. He was a Socialist. There was a Jewish-Socialist Union, called the Bund. He was one of the founders. He had originally intended to go to America. His mother had to smuggle him out of Poland to Germany. He had been exiled to Siberia when he was sixteen or seventeen years old. He eventually made it back to Poland and his mother smuggled him across the border to Germany.
>
> He was apprenticed in Dresden as a *conditor* [pastry chef]. He really intended to go to America and went to Hamburg where he wanted to sail with the Hamburg-Amerika Line. He had to wait some days

until the next ship sailed, so he went north to see what it was like in Denmark. He went to the Danish trade union of bakers, whose head-quarters were in Copenhagen, and they had a Christmas ball—and there he met my mother. He stayed and my mother converted from being a Lutheran to the Jewish faith. And then they married and he made Denmark his home. He was very active politically—he knew all the leading Danish Social-Democratic politicians, like Hansen and Hedtoft.

On the eve of Rosh Hashanah 1943 he brought a roast duck home. He thought it would be the last night we would celebrate together. Just when we were sitting down and having a wonderful meal, there was a knock on the door, and outside there was a messenger from Hedtoft who warned us [of the imminent deportation of the Danish Jews]. My father was an editor of a weekly Jewish newspaper in Denmark until the German occupation and he had strong opinions about the Danish Nazis. They knew him very well. There was a nasty Nazi journal that had printed caricatures of my father.

After the warning, we immediately packed our suitcases and went the same night to the home of my maternal grandparents. My moth-er was overwhelmed by the events and had a nervous breakdown. My father decided to leave Denmark with my older sister. She was twen-ty-five years old and a journalist. She was also well known to the Nazis. And I, now sixteen years old, would stay in Denmark with my mother. A place was found where my mother could be hospitalized and get some care and rest. The same underground contacts that brought my father and my sister to a fishing boat bound for Sweden brought my mother and me to a sanatorium. They were young stu-dents who came and transported us. We stayed at the sanatorium for about a month.

On the evening of October 1, our apartment in Copenhagen was empty. Our neighbors later told us that the Gestapo had looked for us, but we had confidence in our neighbors that they would not turn us in. We stayed for a few more days at my maternal grandparents, and then the Danish police issued us new identity papers and ration cards under the name Christensen, which was my mother's maiden name.

My real name was Hannah Krotoschinsky—so we changed our names to Hanne and Emmy Christensen. Some of the policemen would continue to stay in touch with us. There were rumors, like "now they are taking half-Jews," and we would sleep away from home that night. Otherwise we stayed in our old apartment. We took off our old door-sign and got a new one with our "new" name.

The next thing we did, we went to the town hall, where the administration of all the schools in Copenhagen is located. We explained our situation. The head of the school authorities was very old-fashioned, but also very kind. He said, "We will take this girl, Hannah Krotoschinsky; she will leave school, and a new girl, Hanne Christensen, will come in." Then I went to my school the next day, and the principal, who was also the old-fashioned type, took me by the hand, walked me to my classroom and announced to my classmates: "You see here a new pupil: Hannah Krotoschinsky has left; Hanne Christensen has arrived and will take her place." I went to school the whole time during the German occupation. Once in a while, someone called and said, "You must stay at our place tonight" (for security reasons), and we did. No one turned us in, though hundreds of people—the neighbors, the teachers, my classmates, their parents—knew about us.

There was lots of unrest in Copenhagen in 1944—foremost the General Strike and the arrest of the entire Danish police force. The HIPOs (the Danish Hilfspolizei, or auxiliary police) took over. They were Nazis and very aggressive. I was always looking across my shoulder to see if I was safe. But we looked "Aryan." My mother and I were both blond and blue-eyed.

My mother was always kind of nervous, but I never feared that she would break down again and lose her mind. My dad had never made any money, editing his Jewish journal, but he was in the business of supplying the bakers of Copenhagen with the ingredients they needed to bake bread and cakes: flour, butter, etc. He had many, many Danish customers. My mother had his books, and she would call the businessmen he had supplied, and they gave us credit. They were very nice to us. So with the credit and the ration cards we could exist.

We were in contact with my father and sister in Sweden under the name of Christensen. They got our letters and we would get their letters from Stockholm. The letters were censored and we wrote in a kind of code, but we knew that they were safe and that the Germans were on their way out.

The early end of the war was a complete surprise for us: On May 4th, at 9:00 P.M., Denmark was free again. My father and my sister came back a month later. In June I changed my name again: I took my Abitur (final high school exam) under my old name.[1]

In 1944, while Hanne had taken on a new identity, the Danish resistance movement became more widespread and daring. Jørgen Kieler and other members of the *Holger Danske* resistance group who had assisted with the rescue of the Jews now increased their acts of sabotage. During four months they carried out twenty-five actions against factories that produced radio equipment and sights for bombers, steel mills, and a large shipbuilding yard in Copenhagen.

In February 1944, Jørgen Kieler, his brother, and two other members of their group were betrayed and arrested by the Gestapo. They were sent to prison in Copenhagen and were repeatedly questioned until the end of May. "The daily interrogations were an extreme psychological strain," wrote Kieler later, "but I was not submitted to physical torture. I tried to prolong the case. . . . Finally, it was our turn. [Then] a general strike broke out in Copenhagen . . . and all executions were discontinued for the time being."[2]

Instead, Kieler was first deported to a German camp in Denmark, where he met his father and older sister, and then to Germany, where he and his brother ended up in a concentration camp in Westphalia. There they worked with two hundred other Danish prisoners as miners, blasting and digging underground buildings and railroads. Eventually they would be saved by the intervention of Count Folke Bernadotte and repatriated to Sweden.

In the summer of 1944, Copenhagen was in turmoil. On June 6, when Allied troops landed on Normandy beach, a dozen resistance fighters blew up the Globus factory in the outskirts of Copenhagen.

Sabotage: Flames and smoke from German torpedo boat shipyard in Copenhagen. (Photo courtesy of National Archives, College Park, Md.)

The factory produced parts of the V-2 rockets that were inflicting serious damage on London. Sixteen days later, on June 22, the resistance struck the Dansk Riffelsyndikat in Copenhagen's Frihavn. Denmark's only factory manufacturing small arms, antitank guns, and artillery equipment for the Germans sustained a heavy blow. Thousands of Copenhagen residents watched the fire reduce the building to an empty shell.[3]

The city braced for German reprisals. They were carried out by veterans of the *Frikorps Denmark*, under the command of German officers. Within two days, the *Schalburg Corps* struck at targets that were dear to the hearts of the Danish people: They blew up a part of the Royal Danish Porcelain factory and wrecked the student union at the University of Copenhagen. And they set fire to the concert hall, the dance pavilion, and the Glass Hall of Tivoli Gardens, the famous amusement park in the heart of Copenhagen. Tivoli had been a small island of peace in the turmoil of war. Now it lay in ruins. The Danes were enraged.

Werner Best declared a state of emergency throughout the country, setting a curfew from 8:00 P.M. to 5:00 A.M. All meetings and public gatherings were prohibited. In the morning of June 26, twelve hundred dockworkers at *Burmeister og Wain*, Denmark's largest shipyard, sent a letter to Best in which they announced that because the curfew denied them evening hours to tend their vegetable gardens, they would have to finish work each day at noon. The letter was signed by all workers, even those without gardens. By 8:00 P.M. that evening, the center of Copenhagen was empty, but in the suburbs people ignored the curfew to take a stroll and visit friends. There was little garden tending that evening!

The dockworkers at *Burmeister og Wain* went home the next day at noon. Workers in many small businesses and department store employees also talked about going on strike. Suddenly every Copenhagener wanted eight free hours before curfew. In the evening the city center was quiet, but in the suburbs there were many bonfires. In some streets nervous German soldiers shot into the crowd. On the next day, June 28, every important business in the city came to a halt. At curfew time, to keep German patrols from their streets, the people began erecting barricades; in front of each barricade was a bonfire. Swastikas and portraits of Hitler were burned. In one place the Führer was hanged, then burned, in effigy.

The city's streetcar conductors failed to report for work the following day, and all the telephone operators went home. All postal workers went out on strike in the evening. By June 30, all public transportation had stopped, as the last suburban trains moved outside of Copenhagen and were abandoned by their drivers. Enraged, Best ordered all gas, water, and electricity supplies cut off and the Danish state radio closed down. Roads to the capital city were blocked so that no food supplies could reach its people.

On July 1, German military police units from all over Zealand moved toward Copenhagen. The city's mood was ebullient. On a

Angered by arrest, Danes free members of the Resistance from a German prison van. (Photo courtesy of National Archives, College Park, Md.)

main street someone erected a mock tombstone inscribed: "Sweet, Sweet Little Adolf." All the breweries somehow managed to continue production, and beer was plentiful.

Across the Forum, a small boy thumbed his nose at a German sniper. The German raised his rifle, but the youngster ducked behind a wall before the bullet could reach him. Again the boy leaned out, thumbed his nose, and was shot at and missed. After the soldier had almost emptied his rifle, a German officer ordered the shooting to stop, and the little boy, thumbing his nose a final time, ran away.[4]

The Danes never lost their sense of humor. At the height of the strike, the Germans put a couple of armored tanks in the center of the Town Hall Square in Copenhagen. A prankster managed to place a sign at the base of the tanks: *"Sælges"* (for sale). Schoolchildren made a game of going up to the Panzer troops stationed there to ask, "Where can we buy raffle tickets to win these tanks?"

At night, thousands of bonfires burned in the barricaded streets, many of them lit by old ladies. For the first time during the occupation, Copenhagen was unified in its spirit of resistance. The underground newspaper *Information* put it succinctly: "Score—one for Copenhagen, none for the Germans." But the casualties were high: In the weeklong uprising, 664 Danes had been wounded and 87 killed by German patrols.

During this dangerous situation Georg F. Duckwitz assumed a pivotal role in the strike negotiations. Because of his experience in the shipping industry, he had excellent connections not only with *Burmeister og Wain's* management personnel but also with the striking workers. He had the trust of the leading Danish politicians as well. On July 1, he was picked up by the courier of the Social Democrats and driven to a conversation with Hedtoft, Hansen, and Buhl, the former prime minister, in which they hammered out an agreement to end the strike.[5]

On Sunday, July 2, the Danish officials and trade and industrial council representatives urged the workers to end the strike. But the Freedom Council, representing the resistance movement, continued to support the strike, saying it would do so until the Germans removed the hated *Schalburg Corps* from the city and ended the shooting of innocent civilians. Duckwitz, in turn, challenged Best to prevent future casualties: "If old people and women and children will be killed, what will history say?" he argued.

Annemarie Duckwitz wrote later in her memoirs. "Mein Mann, wie ein Besessener, kämpfte bis es ihm endlich gelang, seinen Vorgesetzten Vernunft beizubringen" (My husband fought, like one possessed, to reason with his superior). Best finally agreed to the Danish demands: He would withdraw the hated *Schalburg Corps* and the armed German patrols from the streets of Copenhagen.[6]

On July 3, in the garden of the Royal Library, members of the Freedom Council drafted the following proclamation: "The concessions from the Germans are so significant that the Freedom Council does not hesitate to urge the population . . . to resume work. This people's strike has shown the Germans that the Danish people will not let itself be threatened or terrorized."

On the next day, July 4, 1944, the city went peacefully back to work. One week later, as suggested by the Freedom Council, the citizens of Copenhagen commemorated their victory with two minutes of silence at noon. Bouquets of flowers appeared on the sidewalks to mark places where people had been killed. People tipped their hats as they passed the wreaths lying on the streets, which bore such inscriptions as the one in the middle of a busy traffic intersection: "To the memory of three Danes who fell here." Nine-year-old Anne Ipsen watched and wondered: "How could an unarmed, orderly, polite people win against an army by just saying no?"[7]

On July 20, 1944, German officers attempted the assassination of Hitler in his headquarters at the Eastern Front. The attempt failed and resulted in the execution of some of Duckwitz's closest contacts in Berlin: Ulrich von Hassel, Adam von Trott zu Soltz, Fritz-Dietrich Graf von der Schulenburg, and Colonel Georg Hansen. Entries in Duckwitz's diary and daybook and the memoirs of his wife, Annemarie, indicate that he had been operating at the periphery of a network of coconspirators who were in opposition to the Führer and his destructive policies.[8]

The days after the failed assassination attempt were filled with anxiety for Duckwitz and his wife. Annemarie writes in her memoirs that her husband was always carrying a revolver and that they were given (cyanide?) pills by their Danish friends in case he was arrested by the Gestapo. In the first days of September, Annemarie Duckwitz was ordered to leave Denmark and go to Germany. Her husband went to the Swedish ambassador for help. Under the pretext of a serious illness that needed immediate medical attention, Annemarie Duckwitz (who was a Swiss citizen) was given a visa to Sweden.

She left in the evening of September 5, 1944—Duckwitz accompanied her to the ferry under the watchful eyes of the Gestapo. Her diary entry on September 9, after her safe arrival in Sweden, is filled with anxiety and questions about the future: "What will happen now?

Will German patriots have another opportunity to assassinate Hitler? Or will the regime of terror by the Nazis demand many more sacrifices? Will Denmark have to suffer more before it will become independent and free again? Will our Danish friends be able to save themselves? Will my husband survive the chaos to come?"[9]

Werner Best, meanwhile, pondered the lessons learned from the general strike in Copenhagen: He knew now that the Freedom Council had consolidated its position with the general public and that even the Danish police were suspect, for they had refrained from acting against the strikers. To keep control, he would have to act against the *one* organized Danish force that could be used against Germany— the country's nine thousand policemen.

In September, Best ordered SS and German police troops to disband the Danish police force, take over all police duties in the country, and deport to German concentration camps those policemen considered most likely to join the Resistance. The raids took place on September 19, 1944, under the cover of false air raid warnings that sounded in Copenhagen, Aarhus, Aalborg, and Odense around noon. While the sirens were wailing, German troop units in trucks pulled up outside police headquarters and substations. The soldiers dismounted quickly and surprised the men inside. By the end of the day, more than nine thousand policemen and border guards had been arrested or, in the case of rural police, disarmed and sent home.[10]

Knud Dyby, who had been active in helping Danish Jews escape to Sweden, narrowly escaped arrest, since he was off duty that day. When he answered the call of the air raid sirens, he saw that his police station was surrounded by German soldiers, so he went "underground," taking with him sacks of forms for passports, birth certificates, and identification cards. He was lucky: He and the other officers who escaped the Nazis technically remained on the police force and continued to receive their salaries from the government. Though he could no longer serve in an official capacity, Dyby would now devote himself fully to the work of the Resistance.[11]

John Meilstrup Olsen was not so lucky. At age thirty-one, he had been sent from active duty on the streets of Copenhagen to the Police

Academy to receive advanced training. He was arrested on September 19 and deported to Germany that same night—together with two thousand other men from the Copenhagen police force. Vans carried them in long silent convoys to Frihavn, where they were herded aboard the steamer *La Plata*. The ship sailed that night, and John would spend the next three and one-half months in Buchenwald Concentration Camp before being transferred to a succession of prisoner-of-war camps in the early months of 1945.[12]

Of the police and border guards, several hundred were imprisoned in Denmark. The bulk of the force, mostly those over fifty-five and those who served rural communities, were allowed to remain at liberty, as long as they did not bear arms or engage in any organized activity against the occupation force. From September 20, 1944, on, the only Danish police seen in uniform in the country were those whom Werner Best permitted to stand guard outside King Christian's residence at Amalienborg. Their function was purely decorative.

Meanwhile Inger Olsen, John's twenty-one-year-old wife, was left to fend for herself and her eight-month-old daughter, Susie. It would take three-and-a-half weeks before she could find out through the Red Cross where her husband was imprisoned. His first letter, written on October 8, 1944, bore Olsen's prison number and a postage stamp with the profile of Adolf Hitler. It also contained a set of "camp rules" from the commander of Buchenwald and instructions to write in German—no doubt to facilitate the job of the censor, whose marks could be seen on each piece of correspondence.

> The date of discharge cannot be announced. Visits to the camp are forbidden. Inquiries are useless.
>
> Excerpts from the camp rules:
>
> Every prisoner is allowed to receive and send two letters or postcards per month.
>
> Incoming letters are not permitted to exceed four pages and sixteen lines and must be clear and legible. Money can only be sent by postal order that contains the first and last name of the prisoner, his birth date, and his prisoner number, but no additional messages.

It is not permitted to enclose money, photos, or newspaper clippings in the letters.

Mail that does not conform to these demands will not be accepted. Hard to read letters will be destroyed. Everything can be bought in the camp. National-Socialist newspapers are permitted, but they must be ordered by the prisoner in the concentration camp.

Food packages can be received at any time and in any quantity.

The Camp Commander
Concentration Camp
Buchenwald-Weimar
November 14, 1944

For three months, Inger and John wrote to each other in the language of the enemy.

My dear Inger and Susie:

First I thank you for the Red Cross Packages. They contain exactly what I wanted.

I miss you both terribly, but I hope it won't take too long until we are together again.

I thank you from all my heart. I hope you manage the best you can and I am looking forward to see our country again. Please give my love to your mother and your sister.

You have to promise me not to lose courage. I hope you have enough money. Susie must have grown a lot, and by now she must be able to walk. I love you.

Your John[13]

Inger Olsen made do as best she could with the help of her mother, who moved into her home to assist her with her infant daughter, and with the support of her older sister, who lived close by. Every month she would go to a local department store *(Havemann)* in Copenhagen, where she would receive her husband's regular salary and his ration cards, courtesy of the Danish government. Whenever possible, she sent packages to her husband via the Danish Red Cross.

With the disbanding of the Danish police, lawlessness spread through the country, and the crime rate increased sharply. So did acts of sabotage by the Danish Resistance. Toward the end of September, Kim Malthe-Bruun, who had signed on as a merchant seaman when he was eighteen, left the life he loved at sea and joined the partisans. He had kept a diary of what he had seen of the Nazi persecution of Jews when his ship docked in various ports of Europe. He was deeply troubled by his observations. This is what he saw in Lübeck, Germany:

> I'll never be able to forget [the poster of] an ugly face reflected in a hand mirror, looking very much like a rat. . . . Almost in relief is an angular, Semitic nose and the caption under the poster reads: "Look at yourself in the mirror. Are you a Jew or aren't you?" How rotten all of these people must be in order not to react violently to this. The Germans are like a ripe fruit that has been damaged and now the rottenness has come to the surface.

In November 1944, after he had joined the underground to help stop the German oppression, Kim wrote: "[We are] living for the moment only and with our lives at stake. The group with which I am working has completely accepted this."

Three weeks later, in mid-December, Malthe-Bruun was arrested by the Gestapo in an apartment in which he was hiding—together with two of his friends in the underground. He was unarmed. He was placed in a maximum security prison in Copenhagen in a cell with five other young men from the Resistance. From Vestre Prison, Kim wrote a Christmas letter to his mother:

Vestre Prison, German Section, Cell 252
21 December 1944

Dear Mother,
    Everything is just fine, and I'm getting adjusted to my new life much better than I had expected. This is certainly a great change, with entirely

new impressions, but there is undoubtedly a lot to be learned from it all.
Many times during the past two days I've thought how wonderful it was to
live at home with you and enjoy all the things home has to give. I've also
been hoping that you are feeling as calm and confident as I am. There are
so many things which you can see and understand only after being separat-
ed from others. . . . Please don't worry. I'll be back home again before long.

I wish you all a Merry Christmas and a very Happy New Year. Please
don't let the thought of me spoil your holidays. I assure you that the most
difficult thing for me are my worries about you.

Kim14

Like Kim's mother, Inger Meilstrup Olsen would also receive a
Christmas letter from prison. This one came from Buchenwald
Concentration Camp in Germany. It was written by her husband, and
bore the blue pencil marks of the German censor:

Concentration Camp
Weimar-Buchenwald
December 3, 1944

My dear Inger and Susie:

Many thanks for your letter. It was a relief for me. Here everything is
well, and I hope you are fine, too. Christmas is coming and I console myself
with the hope that I will be home before that day comes. If that is not possi-
ble, then I wish you and the whole family a happy Christmas. My thoughts
night and day are at home with you, and you cannot possibly know how
much I am looking forward to seeing you again. You must believe me that I
will be able to recognize Susie——she resembles her father. In the hope that
everything is fine at home, I send you my best wishes and greetings.

John15

Inger's husband did *not* come home for Christmas. As American
and British bombing raids intensified over Germany and as German
troops were engaged in a desperate effort to defend the German borders in the west from the onslaught of the invading Allied troops,

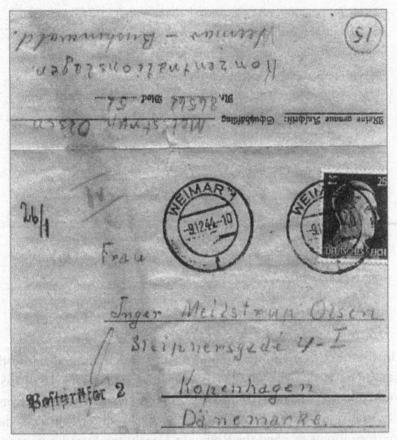

Christmas letter of John Meilstrup Olsen from Buchenwald
Concentration Camp. (Photo courtesy of Inger Meilstrup Olsen)

John Olsen was moved east, from the concentration camp of
Buchenwald, near Weimar, to a prisoner-of-war camp in Mühlberg,
on the river Elbe. His next letter is written in Danish—it bears no
stamp of Hitler and no censor's marks:

P.O.W. Camp Mühlberg/Elbe
January 2, 1945

Beloved Inger and Susie:

　　Happy New Year and thank you for all the good times in the past
year. I hope we will soon be reunited. Thank you for the letter and the

parcel. It was much needed. Please send all the parcels with food that you are permitted to mail; however, the contents must be able to endure the journey. Everything is fine here; please note the new address and [prison] number. I hope you had a good Christmas. Mine was as good as the circumstances allowed. My heart and my thoughts were at home, and during the evening tears came to my eyes.

I can well imagine that Susie has grown. I was really looking forward to see her under the Christmas tree. Soon it will be her birthday. I hope that she still looks like her father. I am now allowed to write in Danish and so are you. It is difficult to write when you would rather talk. I love you—and I have had a lot of time to think things over. . . . You must promise me to take good care of yourself, Susie, and our little home, and then everything will be alright. Give my regards to the family—I hope they are well.

A thousand greetings and kisses,
Dad[16]

In the next four months, Hitler's Third Reich entered its death throes. The Red Army invaded East Prussia on January 16, 1945. From February on, nearly a quarter million German refugees from East Prussia arrived in Denmark. In the last week of February, the American forces reached the Rhine. In March, the Danish resistance leaders asked the British Royal Air Force to bomb Shell House, the Gestapo headquarters in Copenhagen. It contained the largest collection of Nazi files on "underground" activists, and the Resistance wanted it destroyed.

In the meantime, the Gestapo had obtained new evidence against Kim Malthe-Bruun. He was first sent to a Danish concentration camp at Frøsløv, and then back to Vestra Prison—this time in solitary confinement. From witnesses inside the prison, we know that Kim was tortured. Twice he was waiting in a cell at Shell House to be interrogated. He was transferred to police headquarters for further questioning on March 21, the day three waves of RAF bombers headed from England to Copenhagen to destroy Shell House. Within half an hour the building was in ruins.[17]

But the success of the bombing was marred by tragedy. One of the bombers in the second wave of attack crashed into the nearby French School. The building burst into flames. The third wave of planes released their bombs on the burning building, mistaking it for the Gestapo headquarters. Eighty-three children, twenty Catholic nuns, and three firemen died.

Back in Vestre Prison, Kim Malthe-Bruun wrote his last letter to his girlfriend, Hanne. It was April 24, 1945—ten days before Denmark would be liberated.

My own little darling,

Today I was taken before the military tribunal and condemned to death. What a terrible blow this is for a little girl of twenty! I have been given permission to write this farewell letter, but what shall I write?

What do I possess that I can leave you as parting gift so that in spite of your loss you will smile and go on living? We sailed on a stormy sea . . . and we loved each other.

You will live on and you will have other beautiful adventures, but promise me that never will the thought of me come between you and Life.

Lift up your head, my precious love, and look! The sea is still blue, the sea which I loved and which has enveloped us both. Now you will live for the two of us.

Yours, but not for always,

Kim[18]

8

Liberation and Homecoming

Anne Ipsen celebrated her tenth birthday on April 13, 1945. A week later, her father joined a group of Danish doctors to bring back the survivors from the German concentration camps.[1] Among them was John Meilstrup Olsen, who managed to write a letter to his wife, Inger, and baby daughter, Susie, while his train made an overnight stop in the railroad station of Fredericia. They were on their way to Sweden.

> It is going to be strange to pass by so near our home [in Copenhagen],
> without you and I being able to meet. . . . . It can, in my opinion, not be
> long before this senseless situation is over. . . . I have seen many gruesome
> things, and I can tell you [now] that I have been very sick. I had, in
> Buchenwald, an operation on my neck. I lost 30 pounds, so I made a rat-
> tling sound when I walked. [But] I have completely recovered.[2]

A day later, John and the other Scandinavian prisoners, who had been released into Swedish hands, reached the port of Malmö. On April 23 he wrote to his wife: "Promise me not to lose your spirit; that is the worst thing that can happen. Had I lost my spirit, you would have never seen me again. Remember, it will, at most, be fourteen days before this awful time is over." And on the next day: "We are being moved to a camp where we are going to stay for nine days in quarantine. Hereafter we are free men and just have to wait to be sent home."[3]

In quarantine and out of the reach of German censors, John had time to reflect on his experiences in the concentration camps. On April 26, he wrote:

> *Inger, I have received all the parcels that you have sent, including the blanket. It did wonders for me; without it, I would have frozen to death, as it was the only thing that I had. It was a gruesome time in Germany; it cannot be described, but it is luckily behind me.*
>
> *I spent the last two months in a coal mine that was anything but fun. We had no longer any connections to the Red Cross, thus [we received] no parcels. We had in these two months only German cabbage soup and 149 gr of rye bread a day. One was so tired and hungry that it was torture just to get back and forth to the workplace. Moreover, we spent most of the nights in air-raid shelters. It was a wonder that none of us got hurt; the bombs were falling just twenty meters from camp.*
>
> *There was not a day when I did not think of you several times. . . . During the day I followed you in my thoughts. Your letters did wonders. They were read hundred of times; your descriptions of Susie were read [most] eagerly. . . . When I think about her, I feel an awful hate toward the Germans. They have taken away from me the most fun time of her childhood. . . . Remember I love you and the two of you mean the world to me.*

Meanwhile, Hitler's Third Reich crumbled to pieces. On April 30, Hitler presided over his last noon conference in his underground bunker in Berlin. Russian troops were only blocks away. After final farewells to a few intimate associates, Hitler retired to his room and committed suicide.

On May 1 the commander in chief of the German navy, Grand Admiral Karl Dönitz, became the new head of state. To the complete surprise of the submariner, Hitler had designated him as his successor in his will written on April 29. Back in Copenhagen, Georg F.

Duckwitz had learned from his contacts in Hamburg that Gauleiter Kaufmann, the man responsible for the defense of northern Germany, was willing to surrender unconditionally to the advancing British forces. Duckwitz persuaded Best to consider the same course of action for Denmark: A capitulation without a fight would leave the 250,000 German refugees in Denmark unharmed.[4]

On May 3, Best presented his plan to Dönitz in a hastily called conference in Flensburg, the seat of the new German government near the Danish border. Dönitz was receptive. "My policy was simple," he wrote later, "to try and save as many lives as I could."[5] Dönitz ordered an end to the fighting in the north after the British had entered Lübeck on the evening of May 3, and Gauleiter Kaufmann capitulated in Hamburg shortly thereafter.

On May 4, the German High Command surrendered all German forces in northwest Germany, Denmark, and Holland to Britain's Field Marshal Bernard L. Montgomery. In the evening, the news was broadcast in Danish by the BBC. Anne Ipsen remembered:

Just as dusk was falling, at 8:30, the time of the nightly news from England, we heard a crescendo of voices from outdoors. . . . "Germany has capitulated," someone yelled. "We are going to the palace." . . . We ran down the stairs, the three of us hand in hand, so we wouldn't be separated, and joined the thousands of people streaming across Knippel's Bridge toward the palace. . . . We passed a young German soldier standing guard on the bridge. Still almost a child, he stood there with his submachine gun, not knowing whether to laugh or cry, run or shoot. A fellow from the crowd came up and patted him on the back. "Don't worry, now you can go home," he said.[6]

Throughout the whole country, the Danes reacted to the news of the German surrender by placing candles on their windowsills, each household following the lead of its neighbor. From thousands of houses and apartments in Danish towns and villages and from the windows of hundreds of farmhouses the candles broke the night with a soft yellow glow.

For Georg F. Duckwitz, the evening was one of the happiest of his life. His diary entry on May 4, 1945, reads: "Als ich die Nachricht erhielt, hatte ich einen jener seltenen glücklichen Augenblicke in meinem Leben, die mir die wohltuende Gewissheit gaben, nicht umsonst auf der Welt zu sein." (When I heard the news I experienced one of those rare happy moments in my life that assured me that I had not lived in vain.)[7]

On May 5, John Meilstrup Olsen sent a last letter from Sweden to his wife:

> *Today Denmark has been liberated, which means that I will be coming home soon "to my little wife and daughter." Here the day has been celebrated by jubilant crowds, but all my thoughts are at home with you— little Inger. I have spent all my money—22 kroner—but I am sorry all the things that I have bought are for Susie. However, they have promised us another 20 kroner. I would like to buy all of Sweden for you, but you have to settle for silk stockings—if we get the money. Inger! I wish that we were leaving now so that I could be with you tomorrow, Inger! This is all for now. I love you and I hope that you still love me—despite all my flaws. I promise I am going to improve.*
>
> > *Yours,*
> > *John*[8]

Knud Dyby, a fellow member of the Copenhagen police force who had gone "underground," remembered a humorous incident that happened on May 5, early in the morning:

Six o'clock on that . . . morning found me with several Danish Swedish Refugee Service men at Kastrup Harbor to meet a boat with over a dozen foreign newspaper reporters sent to cover Denmark during the Liberation. We were escorting the reporters to Copenhagen, but since we were ahead of the surrender time, I had to negotiate with a German soldier, asking him not to shoot at us just because we were a bit early. I clearly remember his relief in laying his

The people of Copenhagen welcoming British troops. (Photo courtesy of the Library of Congress, Prints and Photographs Division)

gun aside and murmuring, "Gott sei dank!" (Thank God!). The war was over for him and for all of us.[9]

During the previous night, right after the announcement of the surrender, four Danish journalists, stationed at Krusa, decided to move south into Germany to find the British. They drove an ambulance with an assortment of flags. German border guards saluted their passage. The journalists drove all the way to Kiel without running into the British. They finally found the British in Neumünster and presented themselves at 6:00 A.M. on the fifth of May to a sleepy British lieutenant who received them in a four-poster bed. When he was convinced that they were actually Danish journalists who had passed, unchallenged, through sixty-five miles of German-held territory, the lieutenant uncorked a bottle of whiskey in welcome and escorted them to his division headquarters.[10] When the journalists returned to Krusa in the afternoon, they found the frontier station changed: Danish policemen now patrolled the border and thousands of Danes had gathered to welcome the British.

The first troops to enter Denmark were a company of the Thirteenth British Airborne Division, which came to Copenhagen by plane. They arrived on the afternoon of May 5. Major General R. H. Dewing reviewed a company of Danish Life Guards who stood at attention at the airport, greeted representatives of the Danish resistance, and then drove off with his staff to Copenhagen in a convoy of trucks and cars. Cheering residents lined the streets as the convoy headed for the center of town. The reception was the same in southern Jutland where the first British troops crossed into Danish territory around 6:00 P.M. on May 5.

On the same day, the first contingents of the Danish Brigade, whose members had been training in Sweden to fight the Germans in a land battle (which never occurred), crossed the Øresund and arrived in Helsingør. Among them were some of the first Jewish refugees to return home from Sweden: Tove Bamberger's and Mette Shayne's fathers, Fini Schulsinger, and Ina Haxen. But there was no fighting!

Anne Ipsen remembered accompanying her physician father to an Underground Commando Station in a basement restaurant in Copenhagen. "They need a doctor in case there are wounded," her mother had been told over the telephone. "People sat around drinking beer and waited for developments," remembered the ten-year-old girl. "There never were any wounded, but Father examined the throat of one of the freedom fighters. He diagnosed diphtheria and telephoned for an ambulance. The poor man cried, 'For years I have waited for this day, and now I have to go to the hospital with a sore throat!' A roving ambulance drove up looking for the wounded and spirited the patient away."[11]

German troops, as eager to see the end of the war as the Danes, laid down their arms without incident. No violations of the surrender agreement were reported—the withdrawal was orderly. Only on the island of Bornholm, a naval base in the western mouth of the Baltic Sea, seventy-five miles from Denmark, did German forces offer resistance and

A British soldier acknowledging the cheers of joyful Danes in Copenhagen.
(Photo courtesy of the Library of Congress, Prints and Photographs Division)

build up a defense against a possible Russian attack. Commander
Kamptz, the senior German officer on the island, was willing to surrender to the British—a lone British officer landing on Bornholm would
suffice, he told the local Danes—but he refused to surrender to the
Soviet army. But neither British officers nor Danish leaders were willing
to intrude into what was understood to be a Russian operation.[12]

On May 7, in midmorning, Russian aircraft bombed the towns of
Rønne, the capital of Bornholm, and Nesø, on the eastern shore, and
killed nine civilians. In midafternoon, the official German radio
broadcast news of the final German capitulation, which was sched-
uled to go into effect at one minute past midnight on the morning of
May 9. Kamptz still refused to surrender to the Russians.

On May 8, in the morning, the Soviet air command sent fifty bombers over Bornholm. They dropped about fifteen hundred 200-pound bombs. On the very last day of the war, fire and destruction rained upon the island. The Danish radio, expecting the arrival of Field Marshal Montgomery in Copenhagen, paid scant attention to the air raids in Bornholm.

Kamptz followed his orders to the letter. At one minute after midnight, on May 9, he ordered the German troops to step down. The first Russian troops arrived in six torpedo boats in Rønne harbor later that day and landed without opposition. The German surrender was quickly accepted.

The German troops that were leaving Denmark were either elderly soldiers or poorly trained young recruits from the Volkssturm, and men convalescing from wounds they had received on other fronts. Few returned to Germany with any illusions left. In the first days after the capitulation, German units were permitted to take their personal weapons and equipment with them to Germany, where they were subsequently disarmed by the British.[13]

By the middle of May, border control had been tightened. German troops filing down from the north in long columns on the two major roads leading from Jutland to Germany were stripped of their weapons and whatever Danish currency and valuables they carried with them. The typical German soldier was permitted to take home only the clothes on his back and whatever foodstuff he could carry in his knapsack. SS troopers were forced to run—kicked unceremoniously across the border by English soldiers. Ordinary German soldiers walked unmolested into their homeland, which lay in ruins.

On the day of Liberation, a Danish government was formed. It consisted of eighteen members, chosen from the ranks of those who had been active during the war years. Half of the ministers were professional politicians; the others were members of the underground movement. The moment the German army capitulated, the Danish resistance fighters came out into the open. Lists of Danish collaborators with the Germans had been drawn up and mass arrests were carried out.

German troops leaving Copenhagen after their surrender. (Photo courtesy of the Library of Congress, Prints and Photographs Division)

Danish intelligence agents posted on the Jutland-German border plucked out hundreds of collaborators, suspected traitors, German Gestapo agents, and SS officers from the columns of retreating Germans. Within six weeks, twenty thousand arrests were made throughout Denmark.

Official Denmark moved with a vengeance against those who had collaborated with the Germans. On June 1, 1945, a new criminal code was passed that authorized prison terms for persons who had reaped economic rewards from working for the occupation forces or who had lent assistance to the Germans. The code also authorized prison terms for those who had served in German military or police units.

Despite the bitterness against collaborators that erupted in the post-Liberation period, most prison terms, when they were finally handed down, were fairly short. For service in the *Frikorps Denmark,* which fought with the Germans on the Eastern Front—two-and-a-half years; for service as factory guards—two years and eight months;

for service in the SS—two years and nine months; and for service in the Danish HIPO—four years.

Only 15 percent of the twenty thousand arrested in Denmark in the postwar period received prison sentences of more than four years. The death penalty was ordered for seventy-six men and two women. Neither woman was executed, and thirty of the men received reprieves.

Special laws governed public servants: Membership in the DNSAP, the Danish Nazi party, was a punishable offense for government officials. Membership in the DNSAP without other evidence of collaboration was not sufficient cause for criminal proceedings against ordinary Danes. Fritz Clausen, the Danish Nazi leader, was sent to Frøsløv Prison Camp for a period of hard labor. A photo by the Danish Ministry of Foreign Affairs shows him "at work" in banker's clothing, pushing an empty wheelbarrow! Clausen died of a heart attack during a police investigation before the case against him could be concluded.

Toward the end of May and throughout the summer of 1945, the Danish Jews came back from Sweden: Tove Bamberger returned with her mother on May 28. Her father had left on the day of Liberation, with the Danish Brigade, his pockets filled with chocolate for Danish children. Her older sister stayed back in Lund for another month to graduate from high school.

Fifty years later, Tove still has vivid memories of her return: "We all went back on one big boat. . . . I remember being very happy going back. Thousands of Danes were standing on the shore with red and white flags, waving, welcoming us back. . . . And when my sister came back [one month later] her classmates from school came to welcome her in the house. . . . All our stuff was completely where we had left it . . . nothing was stolen. . . . The car my father had bought before the war was still standing there."[14]

And Mette Shayne remembered:

Arriving back in Denmark at the most beautiful time of the year there, with the beech trees just having opened their leaves, I remember seeing my grandfather crying as the train brought us from

Women prisoners of Nazis being led to freedom. (Photo courtesy of National Archives, College Park, Md.)

Helsingør to Copenhagen. The biggest surprise was the huge crowd of people welcoming us home at the railroad station in Copenhagen. Our reception was spectacular.

Among the remarkable things was the care our friends had taken of our belongings. Our home had been used by some underground activists, but was in perfect condition on our return. I remember my surprise at opening my closets in my room and seeing all the things I owned. . . . My father had at the last moment transferred his considerable wine cellar to a friend's house. The friend was very upset that *one* bottle of brandy was missing and kept apologizing for this to my father![15]

Kirsten Meyer Nielsen's family had a grand reception as well: "They had made a portal of flowers across the street [where we lived] and everybody waved and shouted: 'Velkommen til Denmark.' Our house was rented out. We moved into a hotel until the renters had moved out. Everything in the house was fine."[16]

Ove Nathan and his mother experienced an enthusiastic reception in Helsingør: "The homecoming was magnificent. Our apartment was just as we had left it—friends and family had looked after it." Henning Oppenheim remembered: "We had help from many fronts. Our house in Amagar had been looked after by father's former employees." And the people who had moved into some of the rooms in Dan Edelsten's apartment in Fredericksberg moved out as soon as they found another place. "Our apartment was as nice and as well kept as when we fled," he remembered.[17]

The testimony of these six youngsters was typical of the way thousands of Jewish refugees found their dwellings upon their return to Copenhagen and the surrounding suburbs. Neighbors and friends had painted and cleaned their houses and apartments and had filled them with flowers on the day of the refugees' return. Many returning families found that even their household pets and plants had been cared for.

But there were bleaker homecomings as well: Some returning refugees whose houses had been rented out by the government did not feel welcome. Others had lost their lease on their old apartments or found new tenants in them that refused to move. Still others lost their household effects. Some Jews found that their furniture or valuables had been sold to finance the October '43 rescue. In September 1945, 1,300 Jewish refugees were still living in temporary government quarters.[18]

The majority of the returning Danish Jews who had owned businesses or were professionals returned to their former positions. Tove Bamberger's family's business was still run by the same foreman and could count on the same loyal workers that had been employed before they left Denmark. Mette Shayne's father returned to the branch of the same company he had worked for in Sweden. Kirsten Meyer Nielsen's father took over the shoe factory he had inherited from his father. Dan Edelsten's father returned to his position as a physician; Rabbi Melchior returned to his synagogue.

But there were other refugees who had to start from scratch. Silja Vainer's father received no compensation for the tailoring business he had lost. Mogen Adelson's father lost his old job at a shoe factory and had to get by on a small pension and a part-time job. For a while the family received financial assistance from the Central Office for Special Affairs, which assisted impoverished Jews upon their return. The parents of Isak Berkowitz had lost everything—house, household effects, and their business—and had to start all over again. Freddie Vainer's father and grandfather found that the Danish authorities had turned over their shop to their former manager. They had to pay him a large sum of money "for compensation" to get the shop back.[19]

The Jews who returned from Sweden in the summer of 1945 found a new phenomenon in Denmark: The country, which had once united to ensure their safety, was now caught in the grip of searing passions. Questions about patriotism and collaboration were bitterly debated topics, and for a brief period of time, the seeds of anti-Semitism sown during the occupation germinated. On occasion, Jewish families met discrimination when they sought to rent apartments. "They were not happy to see us again," commented a woman who was seventeen at the time. And one man recalled being harassed by his classmates after he transferred from a Jewish elementary school to a public school.

But most of the Jewish children who returned from Sweden and reentered Danish schools made a fairly easy transition. Dan Edelsten, who was seven years old at the time, wrote: "I had started my schooling in Sweden in the fall of 1944 and began school in Denmark after the summer vacation in the second grade. I started out in the Jewish school 'Carolineskolen' [in Copenhagen]. Several of my Jewish friends from the Danish school in Lund also attended Carolineskolen. Many of my classmates were the same [as before]. This meant that starting school in Denmark was very easy. I did not have to make new friends."

Those who had attended the fifth grade in Lund and passed the entrance examination to the gymnasium also made a relatively easy adjustment, since they all began in a new school, like the rest of their classmates who had stayed in Denmark. "I returned to school and easily adjusted," wrote Mette Shayne, who was eleven at the time. "At that age kids do." Some of the older students who attended high school had some temporary problems with language lessons. "It was difficult [for a while]," wrote sixteen-year-old Anita Melchior, "as I had not learned the same subject matter as the other students. However, it went well and I graduated the year after."[20]

Other students, like Ove Nathan, who had graduated in Lund from the Danish school, began their university studies upon their return to Denmark, and Fini Schulsinger, who had begun his medical studies before he fled to Sweden, completed his degree in Copenhagen after his return.[21] Some teenagers were not so lucky: Mogen Adelson had to forfeit school to earn money because of reduced financial circumstances. He found it "difficult to make the transition from the protected milieu of the school to the realities of the business world."

The post-Liberation turmoil in Denmark passed within a few years; the economic situation improved, and the country returned to a more tranquil way of life. The more such normalization won ground, the less anti-Semitism reared its ugly head.[22] To the credit of the Danes, it proved to be a short-lived phenomenon of the immediate postwar period.

Fifteen years after the end of World War II, Rabbi Marcus Melchior reflected upon the homecoming of his people in the documentary film *An Act of Faith*:

> The people of other countries have let their Jews go before, and, per-haps, they were happy to get rid of them, especially when Jewish homes, property, and money were involved. In such cases, saying "Good-bye" was easier than saying "welcome back." But when *we* returned, our fellow Danes *did* say "welcome back." And *how* they said it—emotionally, with open arms and hearts. Our homes, our busi-nesses, our property, and money had been taken care of and returned to us. . . . You cannot imagine how happy it made us feel to be back home.[23]

9

⊗

Getting on with Life

Between 1945 and 1955, three Social Democrats who had warned the Jews in September 1943 about the German plans for their deportation were elected prime ministers of Denmark. Vilhelm Buhl served from May 5 to November 8, 1945. One month after he took office, Denmark became a founding member of the United Nations. Hans Hedtoft was elected twice to the post of prime minister. In his first term, from November 13, 1947, to October 27, 1950, Denmark became a member of the North Atlantic Treaty Organization (NATO). Hedtoft was elected to a second term in September 1953 and died in office on January 29, 1955. He was succeeded by Hans C. Hansen, who served as Danish prime minister and minister of foreign affairs until his death in January 1960.[1]

Count Folke Bernadotte, who had secured the release of the Danish Jewish prisoners from Theresienstadt in April 1945, was appointed in May 1948 by the United Nations Security Council as a mediator in the Arab-Israeli conflict that had erupted after the state of Israel was founded. He succeeded in obtaining an agreement by Arab and Jewish leaders for a four-week truce in the fighting, beginning on June 11, 1948.[2]

But the peace plan that he submitted to the Arab League and the Israeli government on June 28 was rejected by *both* sides. In an ironic twist of fate, Bernadotte was assassinated in Jerusalem on September 17, 1948, by members of the Stern group, an extreme Zionist organization, who opposed his recommendations. Half a century later, when Israeli Foreign Minister Shimon Peres paid an official tribute to the efforts of the Swedish diplomat on behalf of the Danish Jews, peace still eluded Israel and its Palestinian neighbors.[3]

On September 20, 1948, three days after the assassination of Count Bernadotte, the Copenhagen Municipal Court issued its verdict against Werner Best. He was given a death sentence for his actions during the German occupation of Denmark. The court held him personally responsible for initiating the deportation of the Danish Jews in his telegram to Hitler on September 8, 1943. The verdict corresponded to the expectations of the Danish public and the members of the Danish resistance movement.[4]

Werner Best had been incarcerated since May 1945 and had suffered several nervous breakdowns during his three years in prison. An appeal process set in motion by his court-appointed Danish defense lawyer began on May 9, 1949, and ended with a sensation: The Appeals Court *reversed* the verdict of the Copenhagen Municipal Court and sentenced Best to a five-year prison term. The court was *not* convinced that there was clear-cut evidence that Best had taken the *initiative* in the deportation of the Danish Jews.

The second verdict raised a storm of indignation in Denmark. "It goes against the sense of justice of the entire Danish people," according to an editorial in the Danish newspaper *Politiken*. "It is an affront against all Danes who risked their lives against the Nazi occupation." The Danish minister of justice was forced to initiate a new appeal process, which was submitted to the highest court of the land. In March 1950, the Danish Supreme Court issued the last and final verdict—a prison term of twelve years—without any further investigation of Best's guilt or motives!

One and one-half years later, on August 29, 1951, Best won early release from prison. He was expelled to Germany on the anniversary of the Danish uprising in 1943—a coincidence that did not escape the Danish newspapers. He returned to his wife and five children—without any notice in the German press. He spent the rest of his life serving as a consultant for influential politicians in the German Free Democratic party (FDP), working on his memoirs entitled *Dänemark in Hitlers Hand* [Denmark in Hitler's hand]. The book was published in 1988 by Husum Press, the voice of the German-speaking minority in Denmark. Best also served as an occasional witness in the defense of old comrades from the Gestapo.[5]

On July 5, 1989, a West German court in Düsseldorf issued a long-delayed indictment of Werner Best for the murder of 8,723 Poles and Jews in the fall of 1939 when he was in charge of the German Security Police in Poland. But the indictment came too late: Best had died on June 23, 1989, at eighty-six.

Hermann von Hanneken, the infantry general who had commanded the German forces in Denmark from 1942 to 1945 but opposed Best's plan for the deportation of the Jews, was sentenced to an eight-year prison term by the Copenhagen Municipal Court. An Appeals Court reversed the verdict and set him free. He died in 1981, at ninety-one.

Grand Admiral Karl Dönitz became, on May 23, 1945, another prisoner of war. Despite a spirited defense by his American counterpart, Fleet Admiral Chester W. Nimitz, Dönitz was sentenced in the Nuremberg trials to ten years' imprisonment. Following his sentencing on October 1, 1946, he served his time at the Old Spandau prison in West Berlin.

After his release on October 1, 1956, Dönitz returned to Hamburg and completed his *Memoirs*. They were published in Germany in 1958 and in England in 1959. Following old navy tradition, commanding officers of foreign naval vessels visiting Hamburg called on Dönitz as they would on the senior officer in port. He died on December 24, 1980, at eighty-nine.[6]

Georg Ferdinand Duckwitz, the mysterious "Mr. X" of the German occupation, remained in Copenhagen after the city was liberated by the British. He was arrested and remained a prisoner of Montgomery's troops for six hours. The Danish Foreign Ministry and his friend

Captain Schjødt-Eriksen intervened on his behalf, and he was set free. Shortly afterwards he was granted permission to stay in Denmark permanently—in recognition of his "loyal and valuable assistance" to the Danish resistance movement and the Danish citizenry.[7]

Duckwitz returned to his house in Lyngby that had been his residence since 1941. From 1946 until 1950, Duckwitz represented the commercial interests of the West German Chamber of Commerce in Copenhagen. In September 1950, he joined the Foreign Ministry of the Federal Republic of Germany and became the head of the economic section of its new consulate in Copenhagen. In 1953 he was transferred as "consul first class" to a similar position in the Finnish capital, Helsinki.

In the same year, Duckwitz was awarded the Cross of the Commander of the Dannebrog Order by the Danish king, Frederik IX, the son of Christian X, for his actions on behalf of the Danish Jews. On February 28, 1955, Duckwitz returned to Denmark as the new ambassador of the Federal Republic of Germany. His appointment as the chief of the German mission in Copenhagen was warmly applauded by the Danes. Journalist Joachim Bessem, who gained a rare interview with Duckwitz, wrote in the newspaper Die Welt: "He is certainly not one of Germany's most easy-going ambassadors, but one of the most decent ones. . . . He is a man of reason and humanity who preaches only one sermon to his colleagues: 'Please do not take yourself seriously—it is your work that is important.'"[8]

In 1958, Duckwitz was transferred to the Foreign Ministry in Bonn and became director of the East European Division (Ostabteilung). In Copenhagen, Danish Prime Minister H. C. Hansen, a longtime friend of Duckwitz, paid his official tribute to the departing ambassador: "You have represented the true interests of your country in an exemplary manner, with due respect for the opinion of mankind and your host country. There are thousands of Danes who owe you their lives."

Three years later, in 1961, Duckwitz was appointed German ambassador to India and Nepal. Accredited in both New Delhi and Kathmandu, he served as the chief of the West German mission until the fall of 1965, when he returned to Germany and entered volun-

Georg Ferdinand Duckwitz receives the Righteous Among the Nations Award at Yad Vashem, April 5, 1971. (Photo courtesy of Yad Vashem Archives)

tary early retirement. In 1967, Chancellor Willy Brandt called him back to the highest civilian post in the Foreign Ministry of the Federal Republic of Germany. Duckwitz was appointed Staatssekretär—for life—a post of enormous influence where he continued to work with Brandt at strengthening ties between East and West Germany.

In the spring of 1970, on the twenty-seventh anniversary of the Warsaw uprising, Duckwitz was awarded the Heinrich Stahl Prize by the Jewish community in Berlin. One year later, in April 1971, he traveled to Jerusalem, where a tree was planted in his honor on the Avenue of the Righteous at Yad Vashem.

Duckwitz died on February 16, 1973, at age sixty-eight, in Bremen, his hometown. On September 29, 1979, the day that would have been his seventy-fifth birthday, a memorial plaque was unveiled in a room in his former residence, "Friboes Hvile," in Lyngby, near Copenhagen[9]:

> *In this house lived from 1941 to 1953*
> *the German ambassador in Denmark*

GEORG FERDINAND DUCKWITZ
In memory of his action in October 1943
that led to the rescue of the Danish Jews

Duckwitz's colleague, the German chief of shipping in Aarhus, Friedrich Wilhelm Lübke, who had "discovered" an "engine defect" that prevented the ship *Monte Rosa* from transporting Jews to the concentration camps, became, after the war, prime minister of Schleswig-Holstein, the German state that shares a border with Denmark and has a large Danish-speaking minority.[10]

The captain of the *Monte Rosa*, Heinrich Bertram, who conspired with Lübke to keep the ship "out of order" to prevent the deportation of the Danish Jews, became a member of the governing board of a large German shipping company (Norddeutsches Lloyd) in Bremen. In 1970, his company merged with the Hamburg-Amerika Line and became Hapag-Lloyd, the premier German shipping line.[11]

Among the Danes who were officially recognized as "Righteous Among the Nations" at Yad Vashem in Jerusalem are five men and nine women. Among them is Anna Christiansen. Long active in the Women's International League for Peace and Freedom, Anna Christiansen looked after Jewish refugee children who had come to Denmark from Germany and Austria after Hitler came to power. First she enrolled the children in the local school in Nybørg, but after the German invasion, she turned her cellar into a classroom for forty pupils. When the hunt for the Jews was on, after October 1, 1943, she "billeted" the children among her friends in the neighborhood.

One of the survivors, who emigrated to Israel after the war, remembered:

She made sure that every Jewish child was in the care of a Danish family. She inspected the homes to which each of us was sent meticulously. . . . Thus under her personal supervision and vigilance, we were housed by Danish farmers. . . . She disclosed the hiding places [only] to the Danish resistance, so that in the event of danger or her own arrest, the children might be . . . removed to safety. But she did not give up our weekly get-togethers at her own home, ignoring the presence of the Germans nearby and disdaining all risks.

Another one of her charges, now a resident of Haifa, remembered her steadfast warmth and affection: "We have remained attached to her. She revitalized in us . . . our belief in humanity." Altogether forty Jewish children owe their lives to Anna Christiansen.[12]

Missing from the list of the "Righteous Among the Nations" are the names of most Danes who participated in the large rescue operation of the Jewish community in October 1943. The Danish underground association has not divulged their names (even of the principals), on the grounds that it was a collective operation, and the individuals who participated need not be mentioned.[13]

Most of the Jewish children and teenagers who were saved by their fellow Danes remained in Denmark after the Liberation. Some, like Niels and Tove Bamberger, Leo and Gus Goldberger, and Mette Shayne, eventually came to the United States. Herbert Pundik joined the Mahal—the foreigners who volunteered in the Israeli War of Independence; Henning Oppenheim volunteered in Israel during the Six-Day War. Years later, Pundik's son was among the negotiators of the first Oslo accord between the Israelis and the Palestinians.

Today, many of the Jewish children and teenagers who were saved by their fellow Danes are among their country's most prominent citizens: artists, theater directors, teachers, journalists, newspaper editors, librarians, rabbis, professors, psychiatrists, psychologists, public health officials, special educators, and writers. Alex Eisenberg, Leo Goldberger, Hanne Kaufmann, Bent Melchior, Ove Nathan, Ralph Oppenhejm, Herbert Pundik, and Emilie Roi, among others, have written personal accounts of their rescue.

Most feel, as do Isak Berkowitz and John Saietz, that the experience made them more conscious of being Jewish and strengthened their Jewish identity. Wrote Jette Borenhoff: "I am more aware of my Jewish background." Added Mette Shayne: "I did get to know about my Jewish identity, which I did not grow up with." Kirsten Meyer Nielsen commented: "It has given me a notion of what it means to be Jewish. I am neither religious nor associated with the Mosaic society (the Jewish congregation in Copenhagen), but the war has given me a Jewish identity." And Freddie Vainer felt that his childhood experiences had strengthened his belief in the Jewish religion and his ability to survive.[14]

Andrew Buckser writes in his essay "Modern Identities and the Creation of History" that one should not expect a consensus on the meaning of the rescue to emerge among the Danish Jews. Theirs is not a single story, but a chorus of stories in which all attempt to express their individual perspectives of what it means to be a Jew in the Danish society, though the individuals telling their stories vary from being Orthodox to assimilated and secular Jews.[15]

What they have in common is a heightened awareness of prejudice and racism, the plight of refugees, and the potential for abuse of political power in contemporary democratic societies. Mogen Adelson, who was a teenager during the war, learned *this* important lesson in World War II:

> That one cannot take anything for granted. That the order of democracy can only be obtained under normal circumstances. It is difficult to maintain it under other circumstances, as for example war and other crises. All the rights that we had under normal conditions were suspended with a stroke of a pen. They were not formally abolished; the occupying power just did what they wanted. It is therefore important that we, the ordinary Danish citizens, constantly are aware of all kinds of misuse of power that take place in an otherwise democratically governed society where decisions and settlements are made by the bureaucracy. It is important that we have free access to find out what takes place in our government. In this manner, misuse of power can be detected and cited. A free press is one of the most important tools in securing this.[16]

Together with many other Danish Jews, Bent Melchior, successor to his father as rabbi in Copenhagen, considers among the most important lessons he had learned from the rescue "the duty to help refugees."[17] John Saietz, who was a teenager like Bent, when he had to flee with his family to Sweden, became "more positive towards refugees and people who are being victimized and discriminated against" after his return to Denmark.

While grateful to the Danish people for the help he received as a child in those fateful October days, Henning Oppenheim felt that "the Danes [today] ought to be more understanding toward refugees from other countries."[18] And Kirsten Meyer Nielsen expressed her sadness over the increase in racism toward immigrants and refugees in the country she loves. She said:

I wish that everybody [in Denmark] could see the center where I teach. It is a school for hearing-impaired adults—Danes as well as refugees and immigrants from many other parts of the world. At the moment there are students from Somalia, Bosnia, Egypt, Lebanon, Turkey, Taiwan, the Philippines, Italy, Morocco and Iran—all deaf and struggling to communicate with each other and their fellow Danes.

Silja Vainer, like Kirsten, taught children with special disabilities and worked with youngsters who were hospitalized because of chronic illnesses. She feels that her own experience as a small child (one who was temporarily separated from her parents) during the flight to Sweden has made her more sensitive to other people's suffering and more compassionate in her work with mentally ill children.[19] Her husband, Freddie, only four years old at the time of the rescue, also feels a strong commitment to serve others in the practice of community medicine. Having been given the gift of a good life, they both seek to share it with others in need.

Looking back from the vantage point of more than five decades, Niels Bamberger said:

I would say the Danes are great people, and one of the few countries that did more than their share to help the Jews all over the world. . . .

I am sure they would repeat the same thing today if it happened. If it should happen, they would be willing to help with money and their deeds. They are very unselfish and they are not asking for any "thank you" in public by anyone. They never did.[20]

His wife, Tove Bamberger, added: "I love this country for what they did for the Jews. Later on [after the rescue] I realized what other countries had done to the Jewish people, and I realized that it was not necessarily because the Germans were better in Denmark, it was because the Danes were better. So I think that their actions should . . . never be forgotten."[21]

And Mette Shayne commented:

Our countrymen were fabulous. We were in so much debt to them for their help and their courage—to the freedom fighters as well as to our personal friends. . . . Fewer and fewer people are still around to tell the story, and I do feel it is so important to stress how many people put their lives on the line to save our lives and the many instances we were shown humanity and love. . . . Danish Jews have much to be thankful for. Last year I . . . visited Israel for the first time. At Yad Vashem, where you are numbed by revisiting the horrors of the Holocaust, the story of the Danish rescue is like a fairy tale. . . . As a group of Danish tourists were standing in front of one of the boats used for sailing Jews to Sweden, I could not help myself but say to them: "This place must make you proud to be Danish."

Most of the Danish Jews who were rescued as children or teenagers have similar positive attitudes toward the Swedes. Leon Feder wrote, "I feel that I am Danish and a little Swedish."[22] Henning Oppenheim wondered: "What would have happened to us if the Swedes had not shown us humanity and understanding?" And John Saietz is "happy for the way they took us in."

Many are still struggling to come to terms with Germany—its past and the changes that have taken place there since the end of World War II. Some, like Isak Berkowitz, confess: "It is only in the later years that I have come to terms with my emotions toward a nation that caused such an unbelievable amount of misery and unhappiness." Others have not felt like ever going to Germany or having anything to do with Germans. One commented, "I do not like the language and the people who speak it."

Henning Oppenheim *has* visited Germany—frequently. He wrote of his experience: "I know that one should not hold a grudge, and 1945 is more than 55 years ago. However, when I drive through Germany, I always think about what happened there between 1933 and 1945." Others still have a difficult time when they meet Germans, even though, as Hanne Meyer wrote, "I am today aware that the young Germans should not pay for the past."[23]

Dan Edelsten has undergone a transformation in his attitude from negative to positive:

> It is obvious that my attitude toward the "then" Germans is very negative. This is not so much due to my own experience as the notion of the gruesome acts that were committed by that nation in the past. In my then "childish soul" I was upset that it was Japan and not Germany that was the target of the first A-bombs. But I have today a positive feeling for Germany because it is not hiding the past and it fights Nazism and racism in a very forceful manner.[24]

It took Silja Vainer some twenty years to work through her ambivalent attitudes toward meeting Germans, but today she often tells her story to German visitors and appreciates the interest and concern of young Germans—children and grandchildren of the World War II generation—about their country's past.

In some cases a thoughtful parent has helped in the reconciliation process. Ulf Haxen, son of Ina Haxen, one of the few Jews who had been active in the resistance movement, was sent by his mother after the war to a summer camp so he could meet German children.[25] And John Meilstrup Olsen, the Danish policeman who had been a prisoner in Buchenwald Concentration Camp, counseled his daughter Ulla on a trip to Germany not to judge the people of a whole country, but to consider the circumstances under which they lived.[26]

Of all the Danish Jews who have written about the rescue, Herbert Pundik, chief editor of the Copenhagen daily *Politiken*, has perhaps been the most articulate in his plea for recognition of the Germans who were part of the conspiracy of decency that saved his life and that of more than 7,000 of his fellow Danes. His book *In Denmark It Could Not Happen: The Flight of the Jews to Sweden in 1943* includes two chapters in which he tells of the "good Germans " and "the German helpers" who made the rescue possible. "It is naive to believe," he concludes in an editorial in *Politiken*, "that the rescue of the Danish Jews would have been successful if there had not been Germans who saw to it that Hitler's intention . . . would fail."[27]

10

"Whoever Saves a Single Life"

On a windswept hill in Jerusalem stands Yad Vashem, a memorial to commemorate the six million Jews who perished in the Holocaust. It was established in 1953 by an act of the Israeli parliament. Mindful of the Talmudic admonition "Remember the evil and do not forget the good," Yad Vashem also honors "the Righteous Among the Nations," Gentiles who risked their lives to save Jews. To date, more than 19,000 men and women have been recognized with this title. These figures represent only "authenticated" rescue stories. Yad Vashem continues its search for rescuers of the Jews and will do so for as long as necessary—as long as requests are received and supported by solid evidence.[1]

Since 1962, a special commission, headed by an Israeli supreme court justice, has been charged with the task of deciding on whom to bestow this honor. Testimonies are solicited from survivors and from other rescuers, but also from eyewitnesses and, when necessary, from archival sources. When the data on hand clearly demonstrate that a non-Jewish person risked his or her life, freedom, and safety in order to save one or several Jews from the threat of death or deportation to death camps, without exacting in advance monetary compensation, the rescuer is qualified for serious consideration of the "Righteous" title.

The rescue of Denmark's Jewry was unique among the Nazi-occupied countries of Europe. Because so many Danes of all ages, classes, and backgrounds participated in this rescue effort, Yad Vashem, as a special gesture, awarded the title of "Righteous Among the Nations" to the entire Danish people.[2]

In fairness, the Danes were not alone in acting effectively to save their Jewish compatriots. In every nation under Hitler's control, including Germany, there were individual acts of humanity that represented an affirmative answer to the biblical question "Am I my brother's keeper?" But it was only in Denmark that almost everyone, from king to fishmonger, took an active role in rescuing the Jews. Only in Denmark, 99 percent of the Jews were still alive when World War II had ended.

Why were the rescue efforts so dramatically successful in Denmark when they often failed elsewhere? It was not *one* factor alone that contributed to the ultimate success.[3] The survival of the Danish Jews was the product of many interacting factors: their special status in Danish society; the spontaneous cooperation of Danish people from all walks of life in their rescue; the proximity of neutral Sweden, which offered a refuge; the attitude and actions of a number of Germans in the civilian and military hierarchy who saw to it that the Jews of Denmark would not be deported to extermination camps; and last but not least, the timing of the action.

A key factor was the small number of Jews in Denmark—fewer than eight thousand in a population of four and a half million—most of whom lived in the capital city of Copenhagen. Denmark was home to the oldest Jewish community in Scandinavia. The community's origins dated back to 1622, and it had enjoyed full civic equality for centuries. As early as 1690, the Danish parliament rejected the idea of establishing a ghetto in Copenhagen, calling the very concept an "inhuman way of life." And in 1814 *all* racial and religious discrimination was declared illegal in Denmark. Though there may have been some rifts between the "Viking" Jews, the old Jewish families, already fully integrated into the Danish society, and the Russian-immigrant Jews who arrived after the turn of the twentieth century, as an aggregate, *both* groups were accepted by the Danish community at large.

The lack of any notable anti-Semitism and a long history of equal civil rights for *all* had created an atmosphere of tolerance and respect toward the Danish Jews. There was also a large number of intermarriages between Jews and Christians. Many Danish Jews had Christian relatives, and rare was the Danish Jew without a Christian member of the family to whom he could turn in distress—as Hanne Schulsinger did when she went into temporary hiding with her maternal grandparents (and took the Christian name of her mother). If they had no Danish relatives, Danish Jews always had close Danish friends. They were never forced by law to keep to themselves, and they did not do so voluntarily.

Even three and one-half years of German occupation had not altered these conditions for the Danish Jews. The Danish government had insisted on keeping absolute control of its domestic affairs, considering as a high order of priority the enjoyment of full civil rights for all its citizens, including the Jews. Jewish life in Denmark continued essentially undisturbed from April 9, 1940, until the imposition of martial law and the crisis of autumn 1943. No gradual divestiture of rights was instituted by the German occupation force. No requirement that the Jews be identified by wearing the yellow Star of David was ever broached with the king or any government official. Contrary to an endearing and enduring myth, King Christian X never wore the yellow star—because none of his Jewish countrymen did!

Denmark is one of the oldest democracies in Europe. Over centuries, the Danes had developed what they call *livskunst*—the art of living. It was a society where people cared about one another, where individual differences were respected, and where self-reliance, cooperation, and good humor were highly valued. The reaction of the Danish people to the imposition of military law galvanized the country and produced a decisive shift from passive to active resistance.

After August 28, 1943, Denmark was a country without a real government—with its symbolic father figure, King Christian X, under

Oldest Democracies

German guard. In the absence of a duly constituted Danish authority, the Danish people decided to act. For many Danes the rescue of the Jews became a spontaneous act of protest against the German occupation. Doctors, nurses, taxi drivers, students, teachers, and fishermen alike joined the rescue efforts. The king, the bishops, the Supreme Court, the universities, Danish politicians and policemen, the trade unions, and professional and business organizations protested publicly and provided the leadership for many Danes from all walks of life who joined the rescue efforts.

By the summer of 1943, the Danish resistance movement, though small in size, had inflicted damage upon the Germans physically and psychologically and had boosted the morale of the Danish people as a whole. The resistance movement gave the Danes hope and a sense of pride. It also provided role models for ordinary Danes, who were quite suddenly and unexpectedly drawn into their first "illegal" activity: the work of hiding and helping their Jewish friends, neighbors, and compatriots. The rescuers were by and large *not* members of the underground. But many of the "amateurs," suddenly drawn into the month-long rescue effort, continued in the active Resistance until the end of the war.

The rescue was also facilitated by the geographic proximity of neutral Sweden—in some places the trip to safety meant crossing just a few miles of the Øresund. But a key factor in its success was a change in Swedish foreign policy: a turnaround from a more pro-German to a more pro-Allies neutrality. A series of diplomatic maneuvers at the highest levels of diplomacy and government—some involving Swedes and Germans, others involving Danes and Swedes, led the Swedish government to announce publicly, at the beginning of October 1943, its offer of sanctuary to the Danish Jews. That announcement also spelled the beginning of Sweden's generous humanitarian contributions to the safety and sustenance of the Jews.

The significance of the date of the persecutions and rescue—autumn 1943—cannot be underestimated. After the German defeat at Stalingrad and in North Africa, the Danes and Swedes knew that the war had turned in favor of the Allied forces. The battle-weary and wounded German soldiers who had been sent to Denmark to recuperate from their ordeal on the Eastern Front sensed that as well. Young Christian Søe remembered that they joined his Danish family to listen to the broadcasts of the BBC, because they no longer trusted the propaganda from Berlin.

Had the Danes not received Duckwitz's advance warning of the impending raid on the Jews, they would have had little if any opportunity to stage a successful rescue effort. But there were other Germans as well who resisted the planned action. Many of the Wehrmacht troops sent to occupy Denmark were older men, often in their forties and fifties. Unlike younger Germans, they had no great faith in the New Order of the Third Reich.

The harbor commanders in Copenhagen and Aarhus, who put their patrol boats and a ship intended for the transportation of the Jews in dry dock "for repair," were men in their fifties who had served in the German navy in World War I and had seen defeat. After the war, they had sailed the passenger ships of the Hamburg-Amerika Line from Hamburg to New York. They, like the commanding officers of the German naval vessels that were stationed along the Sund, had many Danish friends and were not inclined to pursue unarmed civilians on the open sea. Not a single boat carrying Jews from Denmark to safety in Sweden was seized or sunk by the German navy.

The German army, under the command of General von Hanneken, was equally unenthusiastic about the Gestapo's drive to arrest the Danish Jews. For security reasons von Hanneken opposed Best's plan to rid Denmark of its Jews. The actual roundup of the Jews became the responsibility of the Gestapo and the Danish HIPOs (Hilfspolizei). In several instances, officers of the Wehrmacht refused to cooperate, and according to the eyewitness accounts of many Danish Jews, German soldiers did nothing to prevent their escape to a safe hiding place. Through their nonaction, the Germans created a "window of opportunity" that made it possible for the Danes to rescue their compatriots.

The Danish story teaches us that the possibility of influencing the Germans and their treatment of the Jews existed. In October 1943, the Danes affirmed with their spontaneous actions that in a "civil" society individuals have a responsibility for one another. The rescued Jews, we are told in eyewitness accounts, sang the opening line of the Danish national anthem: *Der er et yndigt land*, when they arrived in Sweden and when they returned home at the end of the war. Translated, it means: "There is a beautiful country." That line had a special meaning for them after their rescue by their fellow Danes.

There was *one* other country in Europe—Bulgaria—that managed to save almost all of its Jews in World War II. It had become a reluctant ally of Germany when it joined the Axis alliance of Germany, Italy, and Japan in March 1941. One-eighth of 1percent of its population, 48,400 people, were Jewish. Most lived in the capital city, Sofia. An additional 11,343 Jews lived in the provinces of Macedonia and Thrace, which Bulgaria had ceded to Serbia and Greece after the end of World War I.

After joining the military alliance with Germany, Bulgaria resumed the administrative control of these provinces. There was, as in "old" Bulgaria, beginning in 1941 and 1942, a slow but steady increase in anti-Jewish measures in those provinces, curtailing Jewish freedom, imposing a curfew, and ordering Jews to wear the yellow Star of David.

But as in Denmark, the Bulgarian population as a whole did not harbor any strong anti-Semitic feelings. Bulgarians had grown up with many ethnic and religious minorities (Armenians, Greeks, Gypsies), and they had lived peaceably with people who had been persecuted during the Ottoman Empire. Besides, the Bulgarian Jews (like the Danish Jews) did not live in separate ghettos. They were neighbors— small vendors, tradespeople, and artisans—people whom one met daily, face-to-face.

When—on German orders—the Bulgarian police arrested the Jews in Macedonia and Thrace in March 1943, their detention did not go unnoticed in "old" Bulgaria, where the Jewish deportees spent several days "in transit" before they were transported to concentration camps, like Auschwitz and Treblinka. Bulgarian eyewitnesses from all walks of life reacted with compassion and outrage.

In his book *The Fragility of Goodness*, Tzvetan Todorov describes the chain of events and the actions of decent people that prevented the deportation of Jews from "old" Bulgaria. The testimony of Stefan, the metropolitan of the Bulgarian Orthodox church in Sofia, was particularly moving. Having witnessed the suffering of the deported Jews from Thrace and Macedonia, he sent a telegram to King Boris III, begging him to stop the deportation. Other church officials spoke out as well. *other religions helping*

Professional and trade organizations—the Bulgarian Writers' Union, the Union of Lawyers, the Union of Doctors, the Union of Artists' Societies, the Craftsmen's Association—sent letters of protest to the king and parliament as well. When Peshev, the vice-chair of the National Assembly, heard of a roundup of Jews in his electoral district, he decided to act. "I could not remain passive—my conscience and understanding . . . did not allow it," he wrote in his memoirs.

Peshev composed a protest letter to the prime minister and, at the next meeting of the National Assembly, circulated it among the other members. He had gathered forty-three signatures when he took his protest to the floor. A motion of censure was passed against him by the opposition, but Peshev refused to resign. He was removed from his post on March 25, but he had won his victory. The king had adopted Peshev's position: The plan for deporting the Bulgarian Jews was abandoned "for the time being."

By mid-May, the international situation had changed dramatically: The Germans had been defeated in Stalingrad, and the Allies were victorious in North Africa. Henceforth, the king would choose to oppose the deportation of the Jews from "old" Bulgaria. The Germans "settled for" the 11,343 Jews from the occupied territories. Only 12 survived the concentration camps.

Reflecting on the rescue of the Bulgarian Jews, one comes to realize that—just as in Denmark—no *one* individual or *single* factor could have brought it about. Only concerted action made it possible. It is highly likely that without the groundswell of public opinion against the deportation of the Jews, the king would not have decided to suspend it. Men of conscience and courage, like Peshev, who was later honored as a "Righteous Gentile" by the state of Israel, would not have acted as they did, if they had not felt that the Bulgarian citizenry stood behind them in their efforts. The Bulgarian people were opposed to the anti-Semitic measures and the planned deportation of the Jews, but a community is powerless without leaders who exercise public responsibility—the bishops of the Bulgarian Orthodox church, the deputies of the National Assembly, the politicians who were ready to accept the risks that their action entailed. "All this was necessary for good to triumph, in a certain place and at a certain time," concludes Tzvetan Todorov. "Any break in the chain and their efforts might well have failed. . . . Good is always difficult, rare and fragile. And *yet* possible."[4]

There was another communal effort that saved the lives of thousands of Jews during World War II. In *Lest Innocent Blood Be Shed: The Story of the Village of Le Chambon and How Goodness Happened There*, Philip Hallie tells the story of a village in southern France where three thousand impoverished mountain people risked their lives for more than four years to shelter about five thousand refugees, most of them Jewish children. No communal effort occurred for this length of time anywhere else in occupied Europe.[5]

The villagers were inspired by the example of their Huguenot minister, André Trocmé, a Righteous Gentile, and his Italian-born wife, Magda. As Protestants, their religious background made them feel close to those who were persecuted. But the rescue mission was not limited to Le Chambon-sur-Lignon. All twelve Protestant parishes on the plateau as well as Darbyists, French Catholics, Swiss Protestants, and American Quakers participated in the effort.

Houses of refuge were established to feed, clothe, protect, and educate the children, who had been smuggled out of internment camps set up by the Vichy government before their parents were deported to concentration camps. By 1943, there were seven funded houses in Le Chambon, mostly located outside the village. They were financed by American Quakers and Congregationalists, the Swiss Red Cross, and even by neutral Sweden. Strangers seeking refuge who "simple decency"

came to the peasants' doors were housed and fed—acts of simple decency that spread from one individual to another.

Even the commander of the German troops, billeted in the nearby town of LePuy, did his part. Major Max Schmehling was a devout Catholic from Bavaria and a high school teacher in civilian life. He counseled his SS counterpart *not* to meet nonviolence with violence.

Denmark, Bulgaria, and Le Chambon, France, shared certain historical conditions that fostered collective rescue operations at the national and local level: Weakness of anti-Semitism and civic equality of the native Jews were among them. Jews in all three countries were assimilated in the broader community. They were accepted by the representatives of the local Christian faith, whether they were Danish Lutheran clergy, Bulgarian Orthodox metropolitans, or French Huguenot ministers. Participation in Jewish rescue efforts was also promoted by membership in social and professional groups that the Nazis had failed to disband and infiltrate, whether they were professional or business associations, students, or groups with a shared moral commitment, like the Quakers.

The relative leniency of the local German commanders also enabled the existing social and church networks to mobilize groups of helpers. Rescue efforts became more sustained and daring as the people of Denmark, Bulgaria, and Le Chambon sensed that the Germans would lose the war—after Stalingrad and the Allied victory in North Africa.

ideas of Allies winning → encouraging

Finally, it was the presence of decent persons in positions of authority who exercised the moral leadership that galvanized communal efforts. Some students of human behavior have begun to investigate how broader *historical* forces and *personal* psychology interacted in the lives of the "Righteous Among the Nations" who were motivated to rescue Jews.[6] Their investigations teach us some important lessons about moral courage under stress and the human capacity to behave altruistically toward other human beings.

Among the most comprehensive investigations of the characteristics and motivation of rescuers of European Jews have been those by Samuel Oliner, a professor of sociology, and his wife, Pearl M. Oliner, a professor of education, at California State University in Humboldt.[7] Samuel Oliner is a child survivor of the Holocaust who was rescued by Polish peasants. As part of their search for the roots of altruism, the Oliners and their coworkers interviewed 682 individuals: 406 rescuers who had been "authenticated" by Yad Vashem, a sample of 126 nonrescuers who were matched with the rescuers on age, sex, education, and geographic location, and 150 rescued survivors. All had lived in Nazi-occupied Europe during World War II. Most respondents were drawn from Germany, France, the Netherlands, and Poland, but there were also rescuers from Denmark in the sample.

The Oliners developed an interview procedure that enabled them to reconstruct the prewar and wartime experiences of their informants as well as their situational and personality characteristics. Their interviews and questionnaire data, systematically and uniformly collected in Europe and North America, allowed for comparisons between rescuers and nonrescuers, including people who claimed to have been active in the Resistance and those who were mere "bystanders."

Rescuers tended to be of four types, each of which was characterized by a cluster of particular experiences, relationships, and values. Each type had some but not all of the characteristics significantly differentiating rescuers from nonrescuers. One group of rescuers reported strong and cohesive family bonds that gave them psychological strength. They were closely attached to their parents, who valued caring for others, dependability, self-reliance, and independent judgment. They tended to have a strong religious commitment. They had a positive attitude toward people in general, had many close friends, and were "good neighbors." Even though they did not live among Jews, they were aware of them and their fate in history, often in the context of their religious teachings.

Another group of rescuers had developed their orientation through consistently close contacts with Jews. Jews were an integral part of their lives. They lived among them, worked with them, and had close Jewish friends while growing up. So did their spouses. Because of their intimate personal relationship with Jews, they were acutely distressed by the Kristallnacht, anti-Semitic propaganda, and the edict for Jews in most European countries to wear the yellow Star of David.

For both of these groups of rescuers a sense of obligation toward others emerged in the context of close personal relationships—family or friends—but for others it emerged from a broad sense of social commitment. One group of rescuers was marked by a strong sense of responsibility for the welfare and improvement of society as a whole. Their relationships with their families or origin varied, but they credited a parent or a "parent figure" with encouraging them to be independent and self-reliant and to practice helpfulness and caring toward people in need who came from different social classes and religions.

A fourth group of rescuers was more abstractly concerned with "egalitarianism." They derived their sense of responsibility from their identification with humanity as a whole and their empathy for people who were suffering. They identified strongly with those who were on the margins of society and regarded themselves as psychologically similar to "out groups," like the Gypsies and Jews. They were moved by other people's pain and felt a strong responsibility to help them. Involvement, commitment, caring, and a strong sense of responsibility set all four groups of rescuers apart from the "bystanders."

Three out of four of the rescuers could be correctly distinguished from the "bystanders" by membership in one of these four groups—those with strong family attachments; those with close Jewish friends; those with broad social commitments; and those with a pronounced sense of egalitarianism. Each identified contributing factor made a rescue action more likely, but the Oliners wisely caution us that we cannot specify the *exact* combination necessary to precipitate such an action on the part of a particular individual in a particular set of historical circumstances.

They remind us that there are important variations in motivations leading to rescue behavior. The majority of the rescuers (52 percent) perceived the act of helping Jews as an affirmation of the value system they had been brought up in, that is, "to love your neighbor as yourself." More than one-third (37 percent) had a great capacity for

value system (Hans stories)
fairytales

more than just principles

empathy and were moved by the distress of those who were persecuted and suffering. Only a small proportion (11 percent) was aroused to rescue actions by principles alone.

toby

More important, it is apparent that the rescuers' commitment to caring did not emerge suddenly in the context of the traumas of the Holocaust. Rather, their preparation for the help they extended to the Jews began long before the rescue action, through the ways they routinely related to others as human beings worthy of respect. "Helping Jews" was less a decision made at a critical juncture in their lives than as a choice prefigured by an established way of life, in their daily actions and habits of living. Many of the rescuers reflected this view, saying that they "had no choice" and that their behavior was simply the "ordinary" or "decent" thing to do.

The findings of Gay Block and Malka Drucker, who interviewed 105 rescuers from eleven different countries and of Eva Fogelman and her staff, who interviewed over 300 rescuers and the Jews they rescued, are very similar: Gender, age, nationality, education, profession, political persuasion, or religious affiliation did not play determining roles as to who would be a rescuer.[8]

★ crucial beliefs ★
no sheep

But Block, Drucker, and Fogelman found in a significant number of cases that the rescuers, as children, had learned five essential principles from a parent, parent surrogates, or teacher: (1) that human beings are basically the same and that differences between them are to be respected; (2) that the world is not divided between "us" and "them," but contains a common bond of humanity; (3) that they should have a clear sense of what is right and what is wrong, and that they should stand up for their beliefs; (4) that they should practice kindness and compassion toward others, and (5) that they should be independent and self-sufficient, and never blindly follow the crowd. Although individual rescue acts were often dependent upon external circumstances, these five principles seem to have shaped the character of many rescuers. They found themselves "bound to all mankind through a common humanity."[9]

Fogelman also noted that many of the rescuers she interviewed had, as children, suffered separation, loss, illness, or deprivation. But

can relate

they had also been exposed to a nurturing adult who encouraged their identification with altruistic role models and showed empathy with people who were suffering or in pain.

For example, Miep Gies, who helped Anne Frank's family in hiding in Holland, grew up sickly and undernourished in post–World War I Vienna. When she was eleven, her parents sent her to Amsterdam as part of an international program to help hungry Austrian children. With that one decision, the young girl lost her home, her family, and everything that was dear to her. But she never forgot the kindness of her adopted Dutch family.[10]

Fogelman's findings bear a striking resemblance to contemporary studies of resilient children who had successfully overcome trauma and adversities in their young lives and who developed into competent, confident, and caring adults.[11] All these children had experienced at least one close bond with a caring adult (not necessarily the biological parent) who was sensitive to their needs and taught them to practice acts of "required helpfulness." These youngsters learned early—usually in middle childhood—that it was important and desirable to help others in need, whether they were vulnerable, sickly, handicapped, or in pain. By the time they reached adulthood, they practiced that helpfulness not only with members of their immediate family but also with old and young in their community.

Mordecai Paldiel, the director of the Department for the Righteous Among the Nations at Yad Vashem, has a special perspective on individuals who saved Jews during the Holocaust. As a child, he and his family were rescued by a French priest, Father Simon Gallay, who sheltered them and saw to it that they could cross into neutral Switzerland. Paldiel has written two books based on the extensive collections of eyewitness accounts profiling the deeds of rescuers that are in the archives he administers: *The Path of the Righteous: Gentile Rescuers of the Jews During the Holocaust* (1993), and *Sheltering the Jews: Stories of Holocaust Rescuers* (1996). They illustrate the altruism, ingenuity, and courage of the men and women who rescued Jews.

From an examination of the evidence at hand, he concludes that rescuers were a much larger phenomenon than many historians of the

Holocaust are prepared to admit. They were not saints, but ordinary people; they rescued Jews not because they were Jews, but because they felt that *every* human being, whatever his or her worth or merit, had a right to life and a decent existence.[12] Paldiel offers these reflections on the "normalcy" of goodness:

> We are somehow determined to view these rescuers as heroes; hence the search for underlying motives. The "Righteous," however, consider themselves as anything but heroes, and regard their behavior during the Holocaust as quite normal. How to resolve this enigma?
>
> In searching for an explanation of the motivations of the "Righteous Among the Nations," are we really not saying: What was wrong with them? Are we not in a deeper sense implying that their behavior was something other than normal? Is acting altruistically such an outlandish and unusual type of behavior, supposedly at odds with man's inherent character, as to justify a meticulous search for explanations? Or is it conceivable that such behavior is as natural to our psychological constitution as the selfish one we accept so matter-of-factly?[13]

The medal awarded to the rescuers by Yad Vashem bears the inscription "Whoever saves a single life, it is as if he had saved the whole world."[14] One interpretation of this Talmudic saying envisions the world as hanging in the balance between good and evil. The decent conspirators from many different nationalities who worked together to rescue the Danish Jews did more than save a single human being—they saved the world. They were imperfect human beings, but they responded immediately and directly to a request for help because it was "the thing to do." They were not indifferent to the plight of their fellow human beings.[15]

By doing what they did in the darkest hours of the twentieth century, the rescuers offer us hope in our own times. In Africa, Asia, the Balkans, and the Middle East, the world, as we know it today, is filled with millions of refugees who are persecuted, uprooted, and made homeless merely because they are perceived as "different"—different because of the color of their skin, their ethnicity, their religious or tribal affiliation. If the rescuers have anything to teach us, it is that in a world obsessed with differences, one can make a difference only by insisting on the essential similarity between all human beings.[16]

In the fall of 1943, in Denmark, men and women and children, too, were able to transcend the prevailing culture of hate and indifference toward those deemed "different." Acts of kindness by ordinary people saved the Danish Jews. It is a lesson that we need to remember and heed today. It is a lesson that saves us from despair. "Every spectacular incidence of evil will be balanced by thousands of acts of kindness," Stephen Jay Gould reminded us. "We have a duty . . . to record and honor . . . these kindnesses when . . . evil threatens to distort our perception of ordinary human behavior."[17]

duty

Selected Chronology

1940

April 9   Germany invades Denmark and Norway.

1941

November 5   Werner Best, the new German high commandant of
               Denmark arrives in Copenhagen.
November 25   Denmark signs the Anti-Comintern act.

1943

February 2   German forces surrender to Soviet troops in Stalingrad.
May   German troops driven from North Africa.
August 28   Werner Best hands Danish government an ultimatum.
               Danish government resigns in protest.
August 29   General von Hanneken imposes martial law. German
               forces march into Copenhagen. King under house arrest
               at palace.
September 8   Werner Best sends a telegram to Berlin saying the time
               has come to deport Jews from Denmark.
September 11   Werner Best tells shipping attaché Georg F. Duckwitz of
               plan to transport the Danish Jews to German concentra-
               tion camps.
September 17   Hitler approves of plan to round up Denmark's Jews.

September 28   Duckwitz informs Social Democratic party leaders of planned roundup of Jews.

September 29   Day before the beginning of Rosh Hashanah, Rabbi Melchior tells Copenhagen congregation of planned roundup of Danish Jews. Thousands go into hiding.

October 1   Gestapo and Danish Nazis carry out manhunt for Jews.

October 9   Fourteen hundred Jews, the greatest number on any single day, arrive in Sweden.

1944

June 6   D Day. The Allies land on the beaches of Normandy. Danish saboteurs blow up Globus factory outside Copenhagen.

June 24   Tivoli Gardens bombed, precipitating strike two days later.

June 26   General strike in Copenhagen lasts a week. Strikes in other Danish cities as well.

September 19   Germans arrest the Danish police. Two thousand are deported to concentration camps.

December 16   Battle of the Bulge begins.

1945

March 21   Shell House, Gestapo headquarters in Copenhagen, is destroyed by RAF bombing. RAF bombers accidentally hit the French school.

April 1945   Scandinavian prisoners, including Danish Jews, brought from concentration camps in Germany on white buses to Sweden.

April 30   Hitler commits suicide in Berlin bunker.

May 1   Grand Admiral Dönitz appointed successor to Hitler.

May 4   German forces in Denmark, Holland, and northwest Germany surrender.

May 9   Unconditional surrender of Germany takes effect at 0001 on May 9. War in Europe ends.

Notes

Chapter 1

1. Harold Flender, *Rescue in Denmark* (New York: Princeton University Press, 1963; reprint, Washington, D.C.: United States Holocaust Memorial Museum), pp. 19–20.

2. Anne Ipsen, *A Child's Tapestry of War: Denmark: 1940–1945* (Edina, Minn.: Beaver's Pond Press, 1998), pp. 5–6.

3. Cited in Richard Petrow, *The Bitter Years: The Invasion and Occupation of Denmark and Norway, April 1940–May 1945* (New York: Morrow, 1974), pp. 159–160.

4. John Oram Thomas, *The Giant Killers* (London: Michael Joseph, 1975), pp. 92–93.

5. Ipsen, *A Child's Tapestry of War*, pp. 51–52.

6. Christian Søe, "A Relatively Civilized War," in *Children in War: Reminiscences of the Second World War*, ed. David Childs and Jane Wharton (Nottingham, U.K.: University of Nottingham, 1989), pp. 161–170.

7. Ellen Levine, *Darkness over Denmark: The Danish Resistance and the Rescue of the Jews* (New York: Holiday House, 2000), pp. 17–18.

8. Royal Danish Ministry of Foreign Affairs, *Denmark: History: The Occupation: 1940–1945* (http//www.um.dk/englisch/denmark/danmarksbog/kap6/6-15.hdm,12/28/1999).

9. Royal Danish Ministry of Foreign Affairs and the Museum of Danish Resistance 1940–1945, *October 1943: The Rescue of the Danish Jews from Annihilation* (Copenhagen: The Royal Danish Ministry of Foreign Affairs, Secretariat of Cultural and Press Relations, 1993), pp. 7–8.

10. Ibid.

11. Bent Bludnikow, "Three Muted Cheers for Denmark," *Jerusalem Post International Edition*, October 1, 1993; Vilhjålmur Örn Vilhjålmsson, "The Greatest Myth," *Berlingske Tidende* (Copenhagen), February 6, 2000.

12. Petrow, *The Bitter Years*, pp. 161–164.

13. Søe, "A Relatively Civilized War."

14. Petrow, *The Bitter Years*, pp. 170–171.

15. Ipsen, *A Child's Tapestry of War*, pp. 49–50.

16. David Lampe, *The Savage Canary: The Story of Resistance in Denmark* (London: Cassell, 1957), p. 4.

17. Knud Pedersen, *Churchill-Klubben* (Copenhagen: Bogens, 1945; 1991).

18. Thomas, *The Giant Killers*, pp. 261–265.

19. Royal Danish Ministry of Foreign Affairs, *Denmark*.

20. Petrow, *The Bitter Years*, pp. 88–193.

21. Børge Outze, ed., *Denmark During the German Occupation* (Copenhagen: Scandinavian Publishing Co., 1946).

22. Rasmus Kreth and Michael B. Mogensen, *The Action Taken Against the Danish Jews in October 1943 with Special Reference to the Conduct of the Danish and German Authorities* (Aarhus: Aarhus University History Institute, 1994).

Chapter 2

1. Hans Kirchhoff, "Georg Ferdinand Duckwitz," in *Tyskere mod Hitler: Fem Diplomater i København* (Copenhagen: Embassy of the Federal Republic of Germany, 1999), pp. 7–24.

2. Hans Kirchhoff, Letter from the Berlin Document Center (20.8.1993), with photographs of documents; Tatiana Brustin-Berenstein, "The Historiographic Treatment of the Abortive Attempt to Deport the Danish Jews," *Yad Vashem Studies* 17 (1986), pp. 180–218; Gunnar S. Paulsson, "The Bridge over the Øresund—The Historiography on the Expulsion of the Jews from Nazi-Occupied Denmark," *Journal of Contemporary History* (1995), pp. 431–464; Vilhjålmur Örn Vilhjålmsson, "Glansen gar af Duckwitz," *Berlingske Tidende* (October 3, 2001), sect. 1, p. 14.

3. Hanna Duckwitz, interview with author, March 2001.

4. Annemarie Duckwitz, unpublished manuscript (courtesy of Hanna Duckwitz).

5. Leni Yahil, *The Rescue of Danish Jewry: Test of a Democracy* (Philadelphia: Jewish Publication Society of America, 1969), pp. 138–139.

6. Georg Ferdinand Duckwitz, *Die geplannte Aktion gegen die dänischen Juden und ihre Verhinderung* (Copenhagen: Rigsarkivet, Duckwitz Archives, 1957; and Jerusalem: Yad Vashem Archives File #027/13); *Die Aktion gegen die dänischen Juden im Herbst 1943—Plan und Durchführing* (Copenhagen: Rigsarkivet, Duckwitz Archives, 1964).

7. Yahil, *The Rescue of Danish Jewry*, pp. 162–163.

8. Siegfried Matlock, *Dänemark in Hitlers Hand: Der Bericht des Reichsbevollmächtigen Werner Best über seine Besatzungspolitik in Dänemark* (Husum, Denmark: Husum Verlag, 1988), p. 117.

9. Yahil, *The Rescue of Danish Jewry*, pp. 153–154.

10. Yad Vashem Archives (Jerusalem: File #027/13–28).

11. Yahil, *The Rescue of Danish Jewry*, p. 165.

12. Richard Camman, biography (Berlin: Die Deutsche Bundesstelle für die Benachrichtigung der nächsten Angehörigen von Gefallenen der ehemaligen deutschen Wehrmacht, 2000).

13. Friedrich Lübke, biography (Berlin: Die Deutsche Bundesstelle für die Benachrichtigung der nächsten Angehörigen von Gefallenen der ehemaligen deutschen Wehrmacht, 2001).

14. Kriegstagebuch der Kriegsmarinediensstelle Kopenhagen. Zweigstelle Aarhus bzw. der Seetransportstelle Aarhus. 7.Oktober–31.Dezember 1943 (Freiburg im Breisgau: Bundesarchiv-Militärarchiv; and Copenhagen: Rigsarkivet, Sp. 9.7222).

15. Johannes Dose, *Georg Ferdinand Duckwitz in Dänemark: 1943–1945*, 2d ed. (Bonn: Auswärtiges Amt, 1992), Referat 012, p. 16.

16. Hans Hedtoft, foreword to *October '43*, by Aage Bertelsen (Munich: Ner Tamid Verlag, 1960), pp. 13–14.

17. Niels Eric Ekblad, "Aufzeichnung über gewisse Ereignisse im Zusammenhang mit der deutschen Aktion gegen die dänischen Juden um den 1 Oktober 1943" (Hamburg, January 22, 1958; Jerusalem: Yad Vashem Archives, File #027/13).

18. Recorded by Rabbi Melchior in the documentary film *An Act of Faith*, broadcast by CBS, December 31, 1961.

Chapter 3

1. Leo Goldberger, ed., *The Rescue of the Danish Jews: Moral Courage Under Stress* (New York: New York University Press, 1987), chap. 8.

2. Andrew Buckser, "Modern Identities and the Creation of History: Stories of Rescue Among the Jews of Denmark," *Anthropological Quarterly* 72 (1999), pp. 1–17.

3. Tove Bamberger, interview (Washington, D.C.: United States Holocaust Memorial Museum, Research Institute, December 26, 1989), File RG-50.030*14.

4. Niels Bamberger, interview (Washington, D.C.: United States Holocaust Memorial Museum, Research Institute, December 26, 1989), File RG 50.030*13.

5. Mette Shayne, personal communication.

6. Marcus Melchior, *A Rabbi Remembers* (New York: Lyle Stuart, 1968).

7. Cited in Leni Yahil, *The Rescue of Danish Jewry: Test of a Democracy* (Philadelphia: Jewish Publication Society of America, 1969), pp. 235–236.

8. Quoted in Herbert Pundik, *In Denmark It Could Not Happen: The Flight of the Jews to Sweden in 1943* (Jerusalem: Gefen, 1998).

9. Leon Feder, personal communication.

10. Marek Halter, *Stories of Deliverance: Speaking with Men and Women Who Rescued Jews from the Holocaust,* trans. Michael Bernard (Chicago: Open Court, 1998).

11. Jette Borenhoff, personal communication.

12. Anita Melchior, personal communication.

13. Pundik, *In Denmark It Could Not Happen,* p. 12.

14. Hanne Kaufmann, *Die Nacht am Öresund: Ein jüdisches Schicksal* (Gerlingen: Bleicher, 1994), pp. 17–94.

15. Hanne Seckel-Drucker, Chapter 7, Josey G. Fisher, ed., *The Persistence of Youth: Oral Testimonies of the Holocaust* (Westport, Conn.: Greenwood Press, 1991).

16. "The Fishmonger and the School Teacher," in Harold Flender, *Rescue in Denmark* (New York: Princeton University Press, 1963; reprint, Washington, D.C.: United States Holocaust Memorial Museum), pp. 182–188.

17. Mogen Adelson, personal communication; Isak Berkowitz, personal communication; Hanne Meyer, personal communication; Allan Philip, personal communication.

18. Emilie Roi, *A Different Story: About a Danish Girl in World War II* (Jerusalem: Yad Vashem, 1990).

Chapter 4

1. Leni Yahil, *The Rescue of Danish Jewry: Test of a Democracy* (Philadelphia: Jewish Publication Society of America, 1969), p. 261.

2. Herbert Pundik, *In Denmark It Could Not Happen: The Flight of the Jews to Sweden in 1943* (Jerusalem: Gefen, 1998), pp. 104–106.

3. Aage Bertelsen, *October '43* (New York: Munich: Ner Tamid Verlag, 1960).

4. Pundik, *In Denmark It Could Not Happen*, pp. 107–108.

5. Knud Dyby, interview (San Francisco: Holocaust Center of Northern California, Oral History Project, June 6, 1991).

6. Niels Aage Skov, *Letter to My Descendants* (Odense: Odense University Press, 1997), chap. 33.

7. Pundik, *In Denmark It Could Not Happen*, pp. 109–112.

8. Anita Melchior, personal communication.

9. Isak Berkowitz, personal communication; Jette Borenhoff, personal communication.

10. Leo Goldberger, ed., *The Rescue of the Danish Jews: Moral Courage Under Stress* (New York: New York University Press, 1987), chap. 8.

11. Kirsten Meyer Nielsen, personal communication.

12. Hanne Meyer, personal communication; Henning Oppenheim, personal communication.

13. Marek Halter, *Stories of Deliverance: Speaking with Men and Women Who Rescued Jews from the Holocaust,* trans. Michael Bernard (Chicago: Open Court, 1998).

14. Emilie Roi, *A Different Story: About a Danish Girl in World War II* (Jerusalem: Yad Vashem, 1990).

15. Herbert Pundik, chapter 4, in Leo Goldberger, ed., *The Rescue of the Danish Jews: Moral Courage Under Stress* (New York: New York University Press, 1987).

16. Jørgen Gersfelt, *Sådan narrede vi Gestapo* (How we cheated the Gestapo) (Copenhagen: Gyldendal, 1945).

17. Preben Munch-Nielsen, interview.

18. Birger Mikkelsen, *A Matter of Decency: The Resistance Movement's Sound Routes from Snekkersten and Espergærde* (Elsinore: Friends of the Sound, 1995), pp. 16–17.

19. John Saietz, personal communication.

20. Tove Bamberger, interview (Washington, D.C.: United States Holocaust Memorial Museum Research Institute, December 26, 1989), File RG-50.030*14.

21. Ibid.

22. Niels Bamberger, interview (Washington, D.C.: United States Holocaust Memorial Museum Research Institute, December 26, 1989), File RG-50.030*13.

23. Ove Nathan, personal communication.

24. Leif Donde, personal communication.

25. Mette Shayne, personal communication.

26. Marcus Melchior, *A Rabbi Remembers* (New York: Lyle Stuart, 1968).

27. Bent Melchior, personal communication.

28. Hanne Seckel-Drucker, Chapter 7, in Josey G. Fisher, ed., *The Persistence of Youth: Oral Testimonies of the Holocaust* (Westport, Conn.: Greenwood Press, 1991), p. 99.

29. Hanne Kaufmann, *Die Nacht am Öresund: Ein Jüdisches Schicksal* (Gerlingen: Bleicher, 1994), p. 126.

30. Ulrich Plesner, letter, *Jerusalem Post*, January 30, 1979.

Chapter 5

1. Hans Kirchhoff, "Doing All That Can Be Done—the Swedish Foreign Ministry and the Persecution of the Jews in Denmark in October 1943," *Scandinavian Journal of History* 24 (1999), pp. 22–23.

2. Herbert Pundik, *In Denmark It Could Not Happen: The Flight of the Jews to Sweden in 1943* (Jerusalem: Gefen, 1998), p. 93.

3. Harold Flender, *Rescue in Denmark* (New York: Princeton University Press, 1963; reprint, Washington, D.C.: United States Holocaust Memorial Museum), p. 241.

4. H. G. Widding, diary, October 10, 1943.

5. Quoted in Josey G. Fisher, ed., *The Persistence of Youth: Oral Testimonies of the Holocaust* (Westport, Conn.: Greenwood Press, 1991), chap. 7.

6. Ulf Haxen, interview with author, September 2000.

7. Ove Nathan, personal communication; Isak Berkowitz, personal communication; Leon Feder, personal communication; Anita Melchior, personal communication; John Saietz, personal communication. (Quotations from the same personal communications are used subsequently in this chapter.)

8. Emilie Roi, *A Different Story: About a Danish Girl in World War II* (Jerusalem: Yad Vashem, 1990).

9. Niels Bamberger, interview (Washington, D.C.: United States Holocaust Memorial Museum, Research Institute, December 26, 1989), File RG-50 030*13. (Quotations from the same interview are used subsequently in this chapter.)

10. Leni Yahil, *The Rescue of Danish Jewry: Test of a Democracy* (Philadelphia: Jewish Publication Society of America, 1969), pp. 357–359.

11. Mette Shayne, personal communication. (Quotations from the same personal communication are used subsequently in this chapter.)

12. Tove Bamberger, interview (Washington, D.C.: United States Holocaust Memorial Museum, Research Institute, December 16, 1989), File RG-50 030*14. (Quotations from the same interview are used subsequently in this chapter.)

13. Kirsten Meyer Nielsen, personal communication. (Quotations from the same personal communication are used subsequently in this chapter.)

14. Hanne Seckel-Drucker, Chapter 7, in Fisher, ed., *The Persistence of Youth*.

15. Marcus Melchior, *A Rabbi Remembers* (New York: Lyle Stuart, 1968), pp. 184–193.

16. Yahil, *The Rescue of Danish Jewry*, p. 365.

17. Jørgen Barford, *The Holocaust Failed in Denmark* (Copenhagen: Frihedsmuseets Venners, 1985), pp. 36–41.

18. Fini Schulsinger, interview with author, March 2001.

19. Dan Edelsten, personal communication. (Quotations from the same personal communication are used subsequently in this chapter.)

20. Jette Borenhoff, personal communication.

21. John Saietz, personal communication.

22. Anita Melchior, personal communication.

23. Hanne Meyer, personal communication.

24. Ove Nathan, personal communication.

25. Mogen Adelson, personal communication. (Quotations from the same personal communication are used subsequently in this chapter.)

26. Eila Rasanen, "Excessive Life Changes During Childhood and Their Effects on Mental and Physical Health in Adulthood," *Acta Paedopsychiatrica* 55 (1992), pp. 19–24.

27. Silja Vainer, interview with author, September 2000.

28. Roi, *A Different Story.*

29. Kirchhoff, "Doing All That Can Be Done," p. 29.

30. Ibid., p. 42.

Chapter 6

1. Herbert Pundik, *In Denmark It Could Not Happen: The Flight of the Jews to Sweden in 1943* (Jerusalem: Gefen, 1998).

2. Jørgen Kieler, *Nordinske lænkehunde: Den første Holger Danske Gruppe* (The Scandinavian watchdogs: The first Holger Danske group) (Copenhagen: Gyldendal, 1993).

3. John Grün, personal communication (Herbert Pundik's Archives). (Quotations from the same personal communication are used subsequently in this chapter.)

4. Martin Nielsen, *Danske i tyske Koncentrationslejre* (Danes in German concentration camps) (Copenhagen: Gyldendal, 1945).

5. Birgit (Krasnik) Fischermann, interview, 1991 (Herbert Pundik's Archives).

6. Ralph Oppenhejm, *An der Grenze des Lebens,* German translation of *Det skulle så være* (It came to pass) (Hamburg: Rütten & Loening Verlag, 1961).

7. Anne Ipsen, *A Child's Tapestry of War: Denmark: 1940–1945* (Edina, Minn.: Beaver's Pond Press, 1998), p. 80.

8. Alex Eisenberg, *Theresienstadt—elegi.* Aarhus: Klim, 1993.

9. Birgit (Krasnik) Fischermann, "Barn i Koncentrationslejr" (Children in concentration camps), *Frihedskampens Veteraner,* 1995, pp. 123–125.

10. Oppenhejm, *An der Grenze des Lebens*, pp. 134–138.

11. Ibid., p. 139.

12. Ibid., pp. 154–155.

13. Ibid., pp. 220–222.

14. Cited in Harold Flender, *Rescue in Denmark* (New York: Princeton University Press, 1963; reprint, Washington, D.C.: United States Holocaust Memorial Museum), p. 222.

15. Cited in Leni Yahil, *The Rescue of Danish Jewry: Test of a Democracy* (Philadelphia: Jewish Publication Society of America, 1969), p. 311.

16. Silja Vainer, interview with author, September 2000.

17. Cited in Richard Petrow, *The Bitter Years: The Invasion and Occupation of Denmark and Norway, April 1940–May 1945* (New York: Morrow, 1974), p. 312.

18. Oppenhejm, *An der Grenze des Lebens*, p. 230.

19. Felix Kersten, *The Kersten Memoirs: 1940–1945* (New York: Macmillan, 1957).

20. Steven Koblik, *The Stones Cry Out: Sweden's Response to the Persecution of the Jews: 1933–1945* (New York: Holocaust Library, 1988), chap. 4.

21. Oppenhejm, *An der Grenze des Lebens*, p. 248.

22. Cited in Yahil, *The Rescue of Danish Jewry*, p. 316.

23. Oppenhejm, *An der Grenze des Lebens*, pp. 249–251.

24. Marcus Melchior, *A Rabbi Remembers* (New York: Lyle Stuart, 1968), p. 196.

25. H. G. Adler, *Theresienstadt, 1941–1945: Das Antlitz einer Zwangsgemein-schaft* (Tübingen: J.C.B. Mohr, 1955).

Chapter 7

1. Hanne Schulsinger, interview with author, March 19, 2001.

2. Jørgen Kieler, chapter 7, in Leo Goldberger, ed., *The Rescue of the Danish Jews: Moral Courage Under Stress* (New York: New York University Press, 1987), p. 153.

3. Richard Petrow, *The Bitter Years: The Invasion and Occupation of Denmark and Norway, April 1940–May 1945* (New York: Morrow, 1974), pp. 275–284.

4. David Lampe, *The Savage Canary: The Story of Resistance in Denmark* (London: Cassell, 1957), chap. 10.

5. Hans Kirchhoff, "Georg Ferdinand Duckwitz: Skizzen für ein politisches Portrait," *Lyngby Bogen*, 1978, pp. 158–162.

6. Annemarie Duckwitz, unpublished memoirs.

7. Anne Ipsen, *A Child's Tapestry of War: Denmark 1940–1945* (Edina, Minn.: Beaver's Pond Press, 1998).

8. Hans Kirchhoff, "Georg Ferdinand Duckwitz," in *Tyskere mod Hitler: Fem diplomater i København* (Copenhagen: Embassy of the Federal Republic of Germany, 1999), pp. 20–22.

9. A. Duckwitz, unpublished memoirs.

10. Petrow, *The Bitter Years*, pp. 288–289.

11. Martha Loeffler, *Boats in the Night* (Blair, Nebr.: Lure Publications, 1999), p. 85.

12. Interview with Ulla Thomsen, John Meilstrup Olsen's daughter, July 2001.

13. John Meilstrup Olsen, letters from Buchenwald Concentration Camp, October 8–November 14, 1944.

14. Kim Malthe-Bruun, *Heroic Heart: The Diary and Letters of Kim Malthe-Bruun, 1941–1945* (New York: Random House, 1955), pp. 349, 351–352.

15. John Meilstrup Olsen, letter from Buchenwald Concentration Camp, December 3, 1944.

16. John Meilstrup Olsen, letter from P.O.W. camp Mühlberg/Elbe, January 2, 1945.

17. Ellen Levine, *Darkness over Denmark: Resistance and the Rescue of the Jews* (New York: Holiday House, 2000), pp. 115–116.

18. Kim Malthe-Bruun, letter from Vestre Prison, April 4, 1945, in Laurel Holliday, ed., *Children in the Holocaust and World War II: Their Secret Diaries* (New York: Pocket Books, 1995), pp. 362–363.

Chapter 8

1. Anne Ipsen, *A Child's Tapestry of War: Denmark 1940–1945* (Edina, Minn.: Beaver's Pond Press, 1998), p. 216.

2. John Meilstrup Olsen, letter from Fredericia, April 22, 1945.

3. John Meilstrup Olsen, letters from Malmö, April 23 and 26, 1945.

4. Johannes Dose, *Georg Ferdinand Duckwitz in Dänemark: 1943–1945*, 2d ed. (Bonn: Auswärtiges Amt, 1992), pp. 20–23.

5. Karl Dönitz, *Memoirs* (London: Weidenfeld & Nicolson, 1959).

6. Ipsen, *A Child's Tapestry of War*, p. 218.

7. Cited in Dose, *Georg Ferdinand Duckwitz in Dänemark*, p. 26.

8. John Meilstrup Olsen, letter from Malmö, May 5, 1945.

9. Quoted in Martha Loeffler, *Boats in the Night* (Blair, Nebr.: Lure Publications, 1999), pp. 110–111.

10. Richard Petrow, *The Bitter Years: The Invasion and Occupation of Denmark and Norway, April 1940–May 1945* (New York: Morrow, 1974), p. 332.

11. Ipsen, *A Child's Tapestry of War*, pp. 220–221.

12. Petrow, *The Bitter Years,* pp. 334–338.
13. Ibid., pp. 342–347.
14. Tove Bamberger, interview (Washington, D.C.: United States Holocaust Memorial Museum, Research Institute, December 16, 1989), File RG-50 030*14.
15. Mette Shayne, personal communication.
16. Kirsten Meyer Nielsen, personal communication.
17. Ove Nathan, personal communication; Henning Oppenheim, personal communication; Dan Edelsten, personal communication.
18. Petrow, *The Bitter Years,* p. 360.
19. Silja Vainer, interview with author, September 2000; Mogen Adelson, personal communication; Isak Berkowitz, personal communication; Freddie Vainer, personal communication.
20. Anita Melchior, personal communication.
21. Fini Schulsinger, interview with author, March 2001.
22. Leni Yahil, *The Rescue of the Danish Jews: Test of a Democracy* (Philadelphia: Jewish Publication Society of America, 1969), p. 381.
23. As told to Harold Flender by Rabbi Marcus Melchior; Recorded in the documentary film *An Act of Faith,* broadcast by CBS, December 31, 1961.

Chapter 9

1. http://www.denmarkemb.org/politi96. "Denmark."
2. http://www.gac.edu/onßcampus/academics/Resources/Library/folke.html. "Count Folke Bernadotte."
3. http://www.lysator.liu.se/nordic/div/folke.html. "Israel Pays Tribute to Sweden's Count Bernadotte for Saving Jews During Holocaust."
4. Herbert Ulrich, *Werner Best: Eine Biographische Studie über Radikalismus, Weltanschauung und Vernunft: 1903–1989* (Essen: J.H.W. Dietz, Nachfolger, 1999).
5. Siegfried Matlock, ed., *Dänemark in Hitlers Hand: Der Bericht des Reichsbevollmächtigen Werner Best über seine Besatzungspolitik in Dänemark* (Husum, Denmark: Husum Verlag, 1988).
6. H. Keith Thompson, "Grand Admiral Doenitz: Last President of a United Germany," *Journal of Historical Review* 20(1), 2001.
7. Johannes Dose, *Georg Ferdinand Duckwitz in Dänemark: 1943–1945,* 2d ed. (Bonn: Auswärtiges Amt, 1992), Referat 012.

8. Joachim Besser, *Die Welt*, January 20, 1958.

9. Cited in Dose, *Georg Ferdinand Duckwitz in Dänemark*, p.13, 45.

10. Herbert Pundik, *In Denmark It Could Not Happen: The Flight of the Jews to Sweden in 1943* (Jerusalem: Gefen, 1998), p. 131.

11. Georg F. Duckwitz, letter to Leni Yahil, January 9, 1958.

12. Vita Laska, ed., *Women in the Resistance and in the Holocaust: The Voices of Eye-Witnesses* (Westport, Conn.: Greenwood Press, 1983).

13. Mordecai Paldiel, letter of April 6, 2001, Department for the Righteous Among the Nations, Yad Vashem, Jerusalem, Israel.

14. Isak Berkowitz, personal communication; John Saietz, personal communication; Jette Borenhoff, personal communication; Mette Shayne, personal communication; Kirsten Meyer Nielsen, personal communication; Freddie Vainer, personal communication. (Some quotations later in the chapter are from the same personal communications.)

15. Andrew Buckser, "Modern Identities and the Creation of History: Stories of Rescue Among the Jews of Denmark," *Anthropological Quarterly* 72 (1999), pp. 1–17.

16. Mogen Adelson, personal communication.

17. Bent Melchior, personal communication.

18. Henning Oppenheim, personal communication.

19. Silja Vainer, interview with author, March 2001.

20. Niels Bamberger, interview (Washington, D.C.: United States Holocaust Memorial Museum Research Institute, December 16, 1989), File RG–50 030*13.

21. Tove Bamberger, interview (Washington, D.C.: United States Holocaust Memorial Museum Research Institute, December 16, 1989), File RG-50 030*14.

22. Leon Feder, personal communication.

23. Hanne Meyer, personal communication.

24. Dan Edelsten, personal communication.

25. Ulf Haxen, personal communication.

26. Ulla Thomsen, personal communication.

27. Herbert Pundik, editorial in *Politiken*, August 4, 1991.

Chapter 10

1. Mordecai Paldiel, *Sheltering the Jews: Stories of Holocaust Rescuers* (Minneapolis, Minn.: Fortress Press, 1996), appendix.

2. Mordecai Paldiel, *The Path of the Righteous: Gentile Rescuers of the Jews During the Holocaust* (Hoboken, N.J.: KTAV Publishing House, 1993), p. 370.

3. Harold Flender, *Rescue in Denmark* (New York: Princeton University Press, 1963; reprint, Washington, D.C.: United States Holocaust Memorial Museum), chap. 22; Leni Yahil, *The Rescue of Danish Jewry: Test of a Democracy* (Philadelphia: Jewish Publication Society of America, 1969), pp. 393–395; Leo Goldberger, ed., *The Rescue of the Danish Jews: Moral Courage Under Stress* (New York: New York University Press, 1987), chaps. 10 and 13.

4. Tzvetan Todorov, *The Fragility of Goodness: Why Bulgarian Jews Survived the Holocaust* (Princeton, N.J.: Princeton University Press, 2001), pp. 3–40.

5. Philip Hallie, *Lest Innocent Blood Be Shed: The Story of the Village of Le Chambon and How Goodness Happened There* (New York: Harper Perennial, 1994).

6. Lawrence Baron, "The Holocaust and Human Decency: A Review of Research on the Rescue of Jews in Nazi-Occupied Europe," *Humboldt Journal of Social Relations* 13 (1985/86), pp. 237–251.

7. Samuel P. Oliner and Pearl M. Oliner, *The Altruistic Personality: Rescuers of Jews in Nazi Europe* (New York: The Free Press, 1988).

8. Gay Block and Malka Drucker, *Rescuers: Portraits of Moral Courage in the Holocaust* (New York: Holmes and Meier, 1992); Eva Fogelman, *Conscience and Courage: Rescuers of Jews During the Holocaust* (New York: Doubleday, 1994).

9. Kirsten Renwick Monroe, *The Heart of Altruism: Perceptions of a Common Humanity* (Princeton, N.J.: Princeton University Press, 1996), p. 184.

10. Fogelman, *Conscience and Courage*.

11. Emmy E. Werner and Ruth S. Smith, *Journeys from Childhood to Midlife: Risk, Resilience, and Recovery* (Ithaca, N.Y.: Cornell University Press, 2001).

12. Paldiel, *Sheltering the Jews*, p. 201.

13. Paldiel, quoted in Black and Drucker, *Rescuers*.

14. Jerusalem Talmud Sanhedrin 23 a–b continues: "For this reason was man created alone."

15. Leonard Grob, "Rescue During the Holocaust—and Today," *Judaism: A Quarterly Journal of Jewish Life and Thought* 46 (1997), pp. 98–107.

16. Patrick Henry, "Why We Must Teach the Rescuers When We Teach the Holocaust," *First Things*, 1999.

17. Stephen Jay Gould, "A Time of Gifts," *New York Times*, op-ed page, September 26, 2001.

Bibliography

Adler, H. G. 1955. *Theresienstadt, 1941–1945: Das Antlitz einer Zwangsgemeinschaft.* Tübingen: J.C.B. Mohr.

Arnold, Elliott. 1967. *A Night of Watching.* New York: Scribner.

Bamberger, Ib Nathan. 1983. *The Viking Jews: A History of the Jews in Denmark.* Brooklyn: Soncino Press.

Barford, Jorgen H. 1985. *The Holocaust Failed in Denmark.* Copenhagen: Frihedsmuseets Venners.

Baron, Lawrence. 1985/86. "The Holocaust and Human Decency: A Review of Research on the Rescue of Jews in Nazi-Occupied Europe." *Humboldt Journal of Social Relations* 13, pp. 237–251.

Bertelsen, Aage. 1960. *October '43.* Munich: Ner Tamid Verlag.

Block, Gay, and Malka Drucker. 1992. *Rescuers: Portraits of Moral Courage in the Holocaust.* New York: Holmes and Meier.

Bludnikow, Bent. 1993. "Three Muted Cheers for Denmark." *Jerusalem Post International Edition.* October 16.

Buckser, Andrew. 1999. "Modern Identities and the Creation of History: Stories of Rescue Among the Jews of Denmark." *Anthropological Quarterly* 72, pp. 1–17.

Dose, Johannes. 1992. *Georg Ferdinand Duckwitz in Dänemark: 1943–1945,* 2d ed. Bonn: Auswärtiges Amt, Referat 012.

Duckwitz, Georg Ferdinand. 1949. "Bag det tyske gesandtskabs kulisser." *Jødisk Samfund,* October.

Duckwitz, Georg Ferdinand. 1957. *Die geplannte Aktion gegen die dänischen Juden und ihre Verhinderung.* Copenhagen: Rigsarkivet. Jerusalem: Yad Vashem (File #027/13).

Duckwitz, Georg Ferdinand. 1964. *Die Aktion gegen die dänischen Juden im Herbst 1943—Plan und Durchführung.* Copenhagen: Riksarkivet, Duckwitz Archives.

Eisenberg, Alex. 1993. *Theresienstadt–elegi.* Aarhus: Klim, 1993.

Ekblad, Niels Eric. 1958. "Aufzeichnung über gewisse Ereignisse im Zusammenhang mit der deutschen Aktion gegen die dänischen Juden um den 1 Oktober 1943." Hamburg: January 22; Jerusalem: Yad Vashem Archives (File #027/13).

Fischermann (Krasnik), Birgit. 1995. "Barn i Koncentrationslejr." *Frihedskampens Veteraner,* pp. 123–125.

Fisher, Josey G., ed. 1991. *The Persistence of Youth: Oral Testimonies of the Holocaust.* Westport, Conn.: Greenwood Press.

Flender, Harold. 1963. *Rescue in Denmark.* New York: Princeton University Press; reprint, Washington, D.C.: United States Holocaust Memorial Museum.

Flescher, Andrew. 2000. "Characterizing the Acts of Righteous Gentiles." *Journal of Religion and Society* 2.

Fogelman, Eva. 1994. *Conscience and Courage: Rescuers of Jews During the Holocaust.* New York: Doubleday.

Friedman, Philip. 1957. *Their Brother's Keepers.* New York: Crown Publishers.

Gersfelt, Jørgen. 1945. *Sådan narrede vi Gestapo* (How we cheated the Gestapo). Copenhagen: Gyldendal.

Goldberger, Leo, ed. 1987. *The Rescue of the Danish Jews: Moral Courage Under Stress.* New York: New York University Press.

Grob, Leonard. 1997. "Rescue During the Holocaust—and Today." *Judaism: A Quarterly Journal of Jewish Life and Thought* 46, no. 1, pp. 98–107.

Hallie, Philip. 1994. *Lest Innocent Blood Be Shed: The Story of the Village of Le Chambon and How Goodness Happened There.* New York: Harper Perennial.

Halter, Marek. 1998. *Stories of Deliverance: Speaking with Men and Women Who Rescued Jews from the Holocaust.* Translated by Michael Bernard. Chicago: Open Court.

Hastrop, Jørgen. 1983. *Passage to Palestine: Young Jews in Denmark: 1932–1945.* Odense: Odense University Press.

Hedtoft, Hans. 1945. "Conscience Must Never Be Neutral." *Arbejdners Almanak* (Worker's Almanac).

Hedtoft, Hans. 1954. Foreword to *October '43,* by Aage Bertelsen. Munich: Ner Tamid Verlag, 1960.

Herbert, Ulrich. 1999. *Werner Best: Eine Biographische Studie über Radikalismus, Weltanschauung und Vernunft: 1903–1989.* Essen: J.H.W. Dietz, Nachfolger.

Ipsen, Anne. 1998. *A Child's Tapestry of War: Denmark: 1940–1945.* Edina, Minn.: Beaver's Pond Press.

Jegstrup, Elsebet. 1985/86. "Spontaneous Action: The Rescue of the Danish Jews from Hannah Arendt's Perspective." *Humboldt Journal of Social Relations* 13, pp. 260–284.

Kaufmann, Hanne. 1994. *Die Nacht am Öresund: Ein jüdisches Schicksal. (The Night Across the Øresund: A Jewish Fate)* Gerlingen: Bleicher.

Kersten, Felix. 1957. *The Kersten Memoirs: 1940–1945.* New York: Macmillan.

Kieler, Jørgen. 1993. *Nordinske lænkehunde: Den første Holger Danske Gruppe.* (The Scandinavian watchdogs: The first Holger Danske group. Copenhagen: Gyldendal.

Kirchhoff, Hans. 1978. "Georg Ferdinand Duckwitz: Skizzen für ein politisches Portrait." *Lyngby Bogen,* pp. 134–179.

Kirchhoff, Hans. 1994. "SS Gruppenführer Werner Best and the Action Against the Danish Jews—October 1943." *Yad Vashem Studies* 24, pp. 195–222.

Kirchhoff, Hans. 1995. "Denmark: A Light in the Darkness of the Holocaust? A reply to Gunnar S. Paulsson." *Journal of Contemporary History* 30, pp. 465–479.

Kirchhoff, Hans. 1999a. "Doing All That Can Be Done—the Swedish Foreign Ministry and the Persecution of the Jews in Denmark in October 1943: A Study in Humanitarian Aid and Realpolitik." *Scandinavian Journal of History* 24, pp. 1–43.

Kirchhoff, Hans. 1999b. "Georg Ferdinand Duckwitz." In *Tyskere mod Hitler: Fem diplomater i København.* Copenhagen: Embassy of the Federal Republic of Germany, pp. 7–24.

Kirchhoff, Hans. 2001. *Samarbejde og modstand undes besattelsen* (Cooperation and resistance during the occupation). Odense: Odense University Press.

Kisch, Conrad. 1998. "The Jewish Community in Denmark: History and Present Status." *Judaism: A Quarterly Journal of Jewish Life and Thought* 47, Spring.

Koblik, Steven. 1988. *The Stones Cry Out: Sweden's Response to the Persecution of the Jews: 1933–1945.* New York: Holocaust Library.

Kreth, Rasmus, and Michael B. Mogensen. 1994. *The Action Taken Against the Danish Jews in October 1943 with Special Reference to the Conduct of the Danish and German Authorities.* Aarhus: Aarhus University History Institute.

Kriegstagebuch der Kriegsmarinediensstelle Kopenhagen Zweigstelle Aarhus bzw. der Seetransportstelle Aarhus. 7.Oktober–31.Dezember 1943. Freiburg im Breisgau: Bundesarchiv-Militärachiv; and Copenhagen: Rigsarkivet, Sp. 9.7222.

Lampe, David. 1957. *The Savage Canary: The Story of Resistance in Denmark.* London: Cassell.

Larsen, Lillian. 1998. "The Letter Kills but the Spirit Gives Life: An Analysis of the Contexts from Which Rescuing/Resistance Behavior Emerged During the Jewish Holocaust." Ph.D. dissertation, Catholic Theological Union (Chicago).

Laska, Vita, ed. 1983. *Women in the Resistance and in the Holocaust: The Voices of Eye-Witnesses.* Westport, Conn.: Greenwood Press.

Levine, Ellen. 2000. *Darkness over Denmark: The Danish Resistance and the Rescue of the Jews.* New York: Holiday House.

Loeffler, Martha. 1999. *Boats in the Night.* Blair, Nebr.: Lure Publications.

Lowry, Louise. 1989. *Number the Stars.* Boston: Houghton Mifflin Co.

Malthe-Bruun, Vibeke, ed. 1955. *Heroic Heart: The Diary and Letters of Kim Malthe-Bruun.* New York: Random House.

Matlock, Siegfried. 1988. *Dänemark in Hitlers Hand: Der Bericht des Reichsbevollmächtigen Werner Best über seine Besatzungspolitik in Dänemark.* Husum, Denmark: Husum Verlag.

Melchior, Marcus. 1968. *A Rabbi Remembers.* New York: Lyle Stuart.

Mikkelsen, Birger. 1995. *A Matter of Decency: The Resistance Movement's Sound Routes from Snekkersten and Espergærde.* Elsinore: Friends of the Sound.

Monroe, Kirsten Renwick. 1996. *The Heart of Altruism: Perceptions of a Common Humanity.* Princeton, N.J.: Princeton University Press.

Moskovitz, Sarah. 1983. *Love Despite Hate: Child Survivors of the Holocaust and Their Adult Lives.* New York: Schocken.

Nathan, Ove. 1998. *Ejne Veje*. Copenhagen: Rosiante.

Nielsen, Martin. 1945. *Danske i tyske Koncentrationslejre* (Danes in German concentration camps). Copenhagen: Gyldendal.

Oliner, Samuel P., and Pearl M. Oliner. 1988. *The Altruistic Personality: Rescuers of Jews in Nazi Europe*. New York: The Free Press.

Oppenhejm, Ralph. 1961. *An der Grenze des Lebens*. Translated into German by Albrecht Leonhardt. Hamburg: Rütten & Loening Verlag. Originally published as *Det skulle så være* (It came to pass).

Outze, Børge, ed. 1946. *Denmark During the German Occupation*. Copenhagen: Scandinavian Publishing Co.

Paldiel, Mordecai. 1993. *The Path of the Righteous: Gentile Rescuers of Jews During the Holocaust*. Hoboken, N.J.: KTAV Publishing House.

Paldiel, Mordecai. 1996. *Sheltering the Jews: Stories of Holocaust Rescuers*. Minneapolis, Minn.: Fortress Press.

Paulsson, Gunnar S. 1995. "The Bridge over the Øresund—The Historiography on the Expulsion of the Jews from Nazi-Occupied Denmark." *Journal of Contemporary History* 30, pp. 431–464.

Pedersen, Knud. 1945. *Churchill-Klubben*. Copenhagen: Bogens.

Petrow, Richard. 1974. *The Bitter Years: The Invasion and Occupation of Denmark and Norway, April 1940–May 1945*. New York: Morrow.

Pundik, Herbert. 1998. *In Denmark It Could Not Happen: The Flight of the Jews to Sweden in 1943*. Jerusalem: Gefen.

Quam, Lori. 1993. "Beyond the Myth of the King and the Yellow Star: Exploring the Reality of the Rescue of the Danish Jews." Senior thesis, Lake Forest College, Illinois.

Rachman, S. 1979. "The Concept of Required Helpfulness." *Behavior Research and Therapy* 17, pp. 1–16.

Rittner, Carol, and Sandra Myers, ed. 1986. *The Courage to Care: Rescuers of Jews During the Holocaust*. New York: New York University Press.

Roi, Emilie. 1990. *A Different Story: About a Danish Girl in World War II*. Jerusalem: Yad Vashem.

Rünitz, Loni. 2000. *Danmark og de jødiske Flygtninge: 1933–1940*. Copenhagen: Museum Tuscalanums Forlag, Copenhagen University.

Silver, Eric. 1992. *The Book of the Just: The Silent Heroes Who Saved Jews from Hitler*. London: Weidenfeld and Nicolson.

Skov, Niels Aage. 1997. *Letter to My Descendants*. Odense: Odense University Press.

Søe, Christian. 1989. "A Relatively Civilized War." In *Children in War: Reminiscences of the Second World War,* ed. David Childs and Jane Wharton. Nottingham, U.K.: University of Nottingham.

Strade, Therkel. 1993. *October 1943: The Rescue of the Danish Jews from Annihilation.* Copenhagen Royal Danish Ministry of Foreign Affairs, Museum of Danish Resistance.

Tee, Nehama. 1986. *When Light Pierced the Darkness: Christian Rescues in Nazi-Occupied Poland.* New York: Oxford University Press.

Thomas, John O. 1975. *The Giant Killers.* London: Michel Joseph.

Todorov, Tzvetan. 2001. *The Fragility of Goodness: Why Bulgarian Jews Survived the Holocaust.* Princeton, N.J.: Princeton University Press.

Vilhjålmsson, Vilhjålmur Örn. 2000. "The Greatest Myth." *Berlingske Tidende,* February 6.

Werner, Emmy E. 2000. *Through the Eyes of Innocents: Children Witness World War II.* Boulder, Colo.: Westview Press.

Werner, Emmy E., and Ruth S. Smith. 2001. *Journeys from Childhood to Midlife: Risk, Resilience and Recovery.* Ithaca, N.Y.: Cornell University Press.

Wyatt, Gretchen P. 1999. "Moral Choice: Citizens and Refugees." Ph.D. dissertation, University of Virginia.

Yahil, Leni. 1969. *The Rescue of Danish Jewry: Test of a Democracy.* Philadelphia: Jewish Publication Society of America.

Yahil, Leni. 1991. *The Holocaust: The Fate of European Jews.* Oxford: Oxford University Press.

Index

Printed in the USA
CPSIA information can be obtained
at www.ICGtesting.com
LVHW030023040324
773396LV00003B/132

9 780813 342788